COMMONSENSE - WISDOM - LEADERSHIP

STEPHEN HISS, MS

ISBN   Softcover   978-1-951469-92-4

Printed in the United States of America.

To order additional copies of this book, contact:
Bookwhip
1-855-339-3589
https://www.bookwhip.com

DEDICATION

To my wife, Pat, for a lifetime of support,
and my daughters, Kimberly and Laura, who, among
many other qualities, posses the heart to be generous, the
strength in self to be fair-minded, and the intellect and
ever-expanding wisdom to appreciate the value of life's
lessons and press forward with their convictions.

ACKNOWLEDGMENTS

Illustrations are provided by Chamisa Kellogg
Kimberly Hiss for providing valuable editing advice
David Fogg; Fogg Management Consulting, for taking personal
interest in this project and providing advice and encouragement
Theresa and Timothy Merkel for their friendship and the
suggestions they graciously gave to strengthen this writing

TABLE OF CONTENTS

FOREWORD

While reading Aesop's Fables to my two daughters years ago, I began to fully appreciate the wonderful lessons they taught about conducting one's own life. Later I became aware of how these same fables provide simple, essential, and powerful guidelines that carry faithfully to many, if not all, of today's management situations. The ten fables I selected beautifully demonstrate how managers can apply knowledge of human nature to achieve the best possible outcome in the workplace.

Management is after all a practice and an art that is applied using those basic management principles and techniques. When they are applied with a measure of commonsense and wisdom the best possible outcome is virtually certain. However, knowing those basic principles, techniques, and philosophies solve "0" operations and personnel problems— like working with mathematical formula, the missing ingredient is how they are applied.

The morals of the ten fables I selected, the case studies taken from my management experiences, and the discussions that follow will not teach new management concepts or techniques. But they do provide something that is essential to everyday management. An opportunity for self-reflection. I have often seen when a manager's assumptions about self-do not match with what their employees and colleagues see. The result of these differences in perception create conflict and misunderstanding that complicates problem solving - and increases a manager's stress level.

Over the years I have observed competent and experienced managers lose sight of the most basic management principles in various management circumstances and especially while under stress - or when short time lines for decision making or action becomes the priority. Unfortunately, these are exactly the times when we need to recall and exercise the management principles we learned and perhaps put aside. I hope you will find the fables, the associated case studies, and discussions not only fun and interesting to read, but worthwhile, and of course, memorable.

Management is an applied art in itself, and when applied successfully to a given scenario, those basic management principles can result in highly successful outcomes. There seems to be a plethora of new management philosophies and techniques that surface each year at seminars and in journals. My experience has shown the most essential elements of strong and successful management have not changed over the last thousand years and are not likely to change in the foreseeable future. The reason for this is simple - human nature has not changed and fortunately, is not likely to change in the foreseeable future. All of which works to significantly increase our chances of success because those same basic principles we learned will apply equally well each day we are on the job. We just have to remember to apply them.

CHAPTER ONE

THE OXEN AND THE LION

A Lion used to prowl about a field in which Four Oxen used to dwell. Many a time he tried to attack them; but whenever he came near they turned their tails to one another, so that whichever way he approached them he was met by the horns of one of them. At last, however, they fell a-quarrelling among themselves, and each went off to pasture alone in a separate corner of the field. Then the Lion attacked them one by one and soon made an end of all four.

United we stand; divided we fall.

Practical Application

A management group will stay strong and unified when its leader appreciates the strengths and weaknesses among its members, works to build competencies, reinforces confidence and trust, provides a clear vision of purpose within the group, establishes clear benchmarks for performance.

Case Study

Dave began his new responsibilities as director of a large division of Manufacturing Inc., and quickly began to see the scope of personnel problems that had been described during the interview process. His managers have been working hard to control a wide range of personnel and operations issues and openly expressed a high level of frustration with Dave during his first operations meeting with them. They were upset and discouraged because it seemed virtually every attempt, they made to correct personnel issues ended with making no progress. When a manager asked an employee to perform a task that was well within their scope of responsibility, the employees felt free to ask the manager why wasn't someone else asked. If an employee made an error that a manager felt justified to address with the employee, the employee would point to the mistakes that others made and ask why he/she was being "picked on." Employees would clock in on time but were slow to be ready to perform the assigned jobs. When one of Dave's managers would attempt a formal counseling, or initiate a written warning, it often failed. Either the HR representative would find flaws in the manager's process or with the documentation. In other situations, the union representative would successfully challenge the counseling. The management group often felt out maneuvered by employees when they attempted to exercise legitimate authority.

It is very evident that the management group was not functioning as a unit, nor did they feel the sense of collegiality that is vital to a high performing group. Further, they felt ill equipped when trying to manage their "foul-spirited" employees. It became clear to Dave that although his managers are hardworking and genuinely motivated to improve operations, their management techniques for handling these problems were inconsistent and ill conceived. Dave also saw little evidence of uniformity with their management practices, philosophies, and techniques. A simple comment by one, "We are being eaten alive," seemed to sum up both their frustrations and the degree of their ineffectiveness.

DISCUSSION

In this case study Dave's managers were willing to take action with employees but in many cases the techniques they used were weak, misdirected, and most often ended in frustration. The case study demonstrates what can happen when a management team attempts to gain control over their work group without a clear central vision and direction from its leader. A lack of good coaching and mentoring resulted in virtual chaos throughout the department. The management team consisted of 12 managers. Most were managers for several years and had been promoted from line positions. None had the benefit of the most basic management training.

A management team is the support system and the department's brain trust. Its members make assessments regarding key elements of the operation. The team functions as change agents for making operations improvements. Its members are the department's overall operations facilitators. Management team members also gauge and represent their employees to the team leader which helps keep the leader operating in the "real world". All of these responsibilities require specific skill sets.

There is a wide range of styles and techniques that successful leaders can apply to build and maintain strong and effective management teams, but among all of these there are a few very important constants that are essential with any management style. A management team leader's central responsibility is to build team strength with coaching and establish a strong central vision that the team's managers can use to guide their decision making and actions. As the *The Oxen and the Lion* fable show, it takes a strong and unified team with a clear vision of purpose and a vision for performance standards and function to overcome a myriad of distractions and challenges. Management team leaders should be able to demonstrate in their day to day work the ten elements that are presented in each chapter of this book which captures the following.

- An ability to appropriately balance organizational expectations with reasonable employee expectations
- An ability to delegate responsibility to the [right] people – at the right time – for the right purpose
- An aptitude for recognizing and accurately assessing failing operations in a timely manner
- An ability to distinguish symptoms from root cause and take appropriate corrective action
- An ability to visualize the critical path to resolving problems while avoiding other distractions and challenges of the day
- Provide appropriate coaching and well targeted manager training programs
- Exercise positive two-way communication with managers and employees

CREATING A BLUE PRINT OR MATRIX FOR DIRECTING OPERATIONS

Management team leaders need to share with managers their points of view regarding management techniques and philosophies. This becomes an on-going process of having one on one conversations and with discussions at operations at operations meetings. It is very instructive to have open two-way conversation during operations meetings about decisions and specific actions taken. Managers on the team will interpret and learn through these open discussions with each other as well. Over time these views create the basis for a central vision which becomes the foundation managers work from to establish performance expectations for themselves and their employees. From Dave's perspective virtually all of this was missing with his management team. The philosophies discussed begin to provide a blue print managers can follow while directing their own operations. When leaders encourage open two-way discussions in a safe and collegial environment about these topics it also works to build a culture of collegiality among those on the team.

Successful leaders can create a positive culture within a management team by providing opportunities for discussion without the threat of retaliation, especially when opinions differ. Working in such an environment will increase managers' confidence as they recognize their skills are maturing and can see they are on more firm ground for making decisions and taking action.

In turn, all of this provides employees with less opportunity to successfully challenge decisions and actions taken by their managers as they sense a more predictable and stable work environment. This consistency also helps employees more easily understand the basis for decisions and actions and are more likely to perform their daily tasks as part of the team. All of this doesn't mean a manger will reach the point of nirvana in the workplace were everyone is thrilled with how their managers and workplace are functioning. It does, however, mean personnel and operations problems are likely to be less severe and when they occur, they will be more manageable. The benefit to the managers, of course, is a less stressful workplace with higher productivity.

KNOW WHEN TO LEAD AND WHEN TO FOLLOW

It's important to appreciate there will be times when team leaders need to recognize there may well be times to follow an alternative or even an opposing view from members of their team. When to lead and when to follow? There are thousands, if not millions of great examples when leaders successfully balanced this management conundrum. Many of our country's most recognized forefathers, American presidents and high-profile business leaders have declared one of their most important traits is being able to recognize times when to take advice from their direct reports. Leadership strength and control is not measured by being [right] all the time, it is the result of being smart – all of the time. And that comes from recognizing one's own limitations weighted [at that moment] against the intellect and vision of someone else. My experience with leaders who view alternate points of view as a challenge to their leadership most often shows they have limitations beyond management skill set. A team leader's own psychological make up combine with their skill set must be sufficiently strong to allow for and consider other points of view without feeling challenged or minimized in any way.

When management team leaders consistently dominate discussions regarding decisions - its managers become disengaged to various degrees depending on the circumstances, and become less likely to exercise their own creativity and problem-solving skills and abilities. I recall one meeting in particular when several vice presidents where engaged in open, creative, and worthwhile conversation until their bigger than life leader entered the room. At that moment all attention centered around their leader and all discussion abruptly stopped. This occurs especially if their leader has a fragile temperament. Sometimes we attempt to excuse these bigger than life and sometimes fragile leaders by pointing to what appears to be their superior intellect. While the assessment may be true, superior intellect on it own may not be an adequate substitute for a lack of character. Most often good managers who work in this environment are much less likely to be creative problem solvers and are often looking for a way out because it minimizes their abilities.

Of course, the other side of that management conundrum is when leaders rely too heavily on consensus. This often leads to inconsistencies with decision making and actions taken. The work environment becomes unpredictable for employees who often spend more time calculating what they need to do to stay whole rather than how they can do the best job possible. The difficulty is that there are very few rules for leaders must rely on exercising their own commonsense, experience, intellect, and wisdom that is gained from learning from past experiences and open conversions.

KNOW THE MANAGERS ON YOUR TEAM

It is important for management team leaders to know their managers. By this I mean get to know what makes each manager tick. What parts of their jobs do they enjoy and excites them? Know the situations that make them feel vulnerable. This provides opportunities to intervene subtly or sometimes more directly if needed to initiate coaching and provide support in advance to help assure to the best possible outcome. For example, get to know how managers view their employees. This is helpful because very often a manager's view of their employees is what ultimately drives their decision making and the actions they are about to take. Leaders can often make this assessment pretty accurately by recognizing a manager's past actions weighted against circumstances. This does not mean management team leaders need to adopt a paternalist approach. It does mean team leaders need to make objective and accurate assessments of their manager's specific skill sets, tendencies, and limitations. It becomes the basis for providing on-going coaching and support. It is also helpful to recognize whether or not a manager's view of him or herself is aligned with those of their employees. It is not unusual for employees to see their managers in a much different light and these differences can be the root of having and on-going personnel problems. Chapters Two and Three address this in more detail.

As we see in the case study, employees can find ways to take advantage of those "cracks" in management's armor and can work creatively to exploit poorly applied management techniques and philosophies. Managers may not be aware of their own underlying belief system regarding employees. I have worked with managers who deep down viewed employees as, "they can't be trusted", or "employees are basically deceptive", or "lazy" or "[they] are only interested in what they can get away with". If these views are held, the manager is more likely to view and manage employees in a heavy-handed, arbitrary, or possibly unreasonable manner - especially when they feel challenged. The most likely extension of this is an unhappy workgroup and a frustrated manager. Let me give one more example, another manager may function with the opposite view and not realize their own strong paternalistic philosophy that leads them to be too concerned about employees' feeling. These managers may not recognize how often they "look the other way" rather than address difficult situations promptly and directly, especially regarding employee performance issues. Still another scenario may a manager who dies not realize how often he / she depends on favorite employee[s] who can be persuaded to perform tasks because other employees can't, refuse, or simply don't like to perform.

Actually, Dave found virtually all of the above aberrations of good management in his situation.

These approaches are problematic enough on their own, but they are often coupled with the manager accepting and rationalizing the situation as status quo. These various dysfunctions can also lead to recruiting problems. Employees communicate freely within their organization and outside in the community about their conditions at work. When these are described unfavorably highly productive employees are much less likely to apply for open positions, and Dave began to recognize this problem when as recruiting efforts failed to attach highly qualified candidates. Positions were vacant for much longer than usual, and for the most part, only candidates with marginal skills and work profiles were applying for open positions.

DEPARTMENT ROUNDS

One way for team leaders' to better understand their managers is by rounding. I would set aside approximately one and a half hours to make rounds. Making general observations of workflow, cleanliness, along with mannerisms and conduct of employees gives important clues about a manager's priorities. Along the way I would talk with employees and hear their views on the various procedures they performed, tasks, and general work flow. By having these brief and casual conversations leaders can see how closely employees link the way they perform their jobs to the organization's mission, objectives, and values. For example, in a healthcare environment an employee may demonstrate their personal pride by describing how they initiated an [extra] personal effort to ease a patient's anxiety. In a workplace that provides customer service, an employee might be happy to point out how something special they discovered and use helps to meet customers' needs in some way. Sometimes employees will take the opportunity to say hello and talk just for conversation sake to tell me about their recent visit with grandchildren. Other times I was curious and asked about a specific task an employee was performing. In all of these occasions I would make sure to say hello and chat for a few minutes with their manager when available. These conversations were not weighty in any way, but they gave employees an opportunity to express themselves in a personal way to management and it gave me an opportunity to learn a little about the nitty gritty of department's daily activity.

My hope in rounding was to hear employees express a measure of pride in the work they do. Pride is a critical element that I look for while observing and talking with managers and employees. When managers and employees demonstrate a sense pf pride in their work it can indicate the operation is healthy and well managed. Pride within a workgroup functions as an essential glue that helps to hold employees together as a team with their manager. When leaders do not hear this enthusiasm or see an element of pride within a workgroup it indicates some amount of follow up may be needed about how things are going in that area. Pride within a workgroup also helps everyone's willingness to work through difficult situations. It creates an environment that encourages managers to reach for making improvements and encourages employees to engage with those improvement opportunities. A sense of pride in the workplace allows the thought that there is always an opportunity to improve the workplace environment in a meaningful way; improve efficiencies or simply strengthen morale.

It is helpful when management leaders talk about their rounding experience during operations meetings [while maintaining the privacy of employees'] discussions. Doing so creates a general picture for all managers on the team to be aware of what is and is not happening throughout the division. This both reminds and encourages managers to continually look for weak points in their work areas and consider opportunities to improve elements of their operation regarding things like employee morale and operating efficiencies. It also works to create a healthy and positive competition among managers on the team.

It is easy and convenient for us to take for granted our operations are doing well in the absence of obvious problems. But, very often it's a little positive adjustment to just an [OK] situation that provides a noticeable difference to employees. Doing rounds of a large department or simply taking time to visit a smaller workgroup, talk with employees, and see exactly how employees perform their tasks yields real long-term benefits. Actually, in the end it is the work group's manager is who gains the most benefit and credit for the outcome of rounding. It's time well spent.

WHERE TO START

Promoting employees from the ranks as was the case with Dave's situation, and expecting them to assume management responsibilities without training or coaching in today's busy, sometimes perplexing, and demanding work environments is a recipe for trouble. This case study had 12 intelligent people who had a great work ethic and potential, but they were very frustrated with their situations. They had no choice but to invent and apply their own perspectives, approaches, and techniques as situations with their employees evolved. The result was the aberrations of good management that are described above. It became very difficult when Dave's managers attempted corrective actions that were driven with those misguided philosophies and techniques. Trying harder as the case study shows resulted in more frustrated.

In addition, their employees were frustrated and angry because they were being subjected at times to what could be considered inappropriate and sometimes "crazy" management tactics. In the case study this anger and frustration provoked employees to react and create new challenges for their managers which brought a continuous circle of passive aggressive employee conduct and reaction from their managers. As a result, virtually all the managers were convinced the root cause of their frustrations was, the employees. Given the situation described in the case study the management team leader had a few critical questions that needed to be answered as soon as possible.

- What specifically needs to be addressed, what approach should be used, what are the priorities for taking action, and what should be the sequence of steps taken? What is the root cause[s] as opposed to the symptoms? What should I do first and how should I do it?

Leaders in situations similar to what is described in the case study will find very early on that there are no silver bullet solutions. Given that there is no defined straight line to [the] action plan that will lead to solving all the pieces of this puzzle, fact finding and thorough assessment is needed not action. Dave also needed to know what if any resources or support are available from this boss. Unfortunately, very often the reality is little - despite earlier offers from senior management to help. That well intended support is often limited. The reality is senior management and Dave's boss hired him to fix the problems and that is the expectation.

Dave needed to use his own experience, past successes and failures, and skill set with time-tested management philosophies, and intuition. He needed to do detailed fact finding and make accurate and timely assessments of cause and effect that would help him visualize the critical path to solutions. Fortunately for Dave he was able to recognize early on a substantial portion of the root cause of the department's problems was with the management team and not the employees. Despite their hard work, well intentioned and genuine efforts to resolve problems, they were simply not equipped to handle their respective situations, and he was also able to see how his managers' employees were able to take full advantage of the situation.

I have found in majority of cases where operations have become dysfunctional, the employees' function more as mirrors that reflect poor management despite cries of management to the contrary. Dave suspected and found that in some situations there were a few employees who were simply "bad apples" and those situations would have to be addressed and dealt with as directly as possible. But for the most part he realized step 1 was to begin coaching and mentoring his managers while offering all the emotional support he could provide. The good news for him was that he also assessed and recognized their potential through one on one conversations and during operations meetings.

KNOW THY SELF

I outlined above the need for management team leaders to know and understand what makes each of their managers "tick". It is equally important for team leaders to have a realistic view of their own strengths, traits, tendencies, and yes, vulnerabilities. "Under what kind of situations do I tend to respond favorably and not." Having an accurate view of one's tendencies when handling various situations is important for the same reasons' leaders should be aware of the thought tendencies of their managers. It's easy to take ourselves for granted and make assumptions about our various points of view regarding employees and management. Making a self-assessment can be uncomfortable, but there are various ways this can be done easily, somewhat painlessly, and with reasonable accuracy. There are simple and free assessments tools online that can provide clues to help recognize our thinking. Management team leaders sometimes use a 360-degree method to get impressions from colleagues. And, sometimes paying close attention to one's self in various situations and later reflect objectively as possible on the situation can be helpful. If there is a particular trait or tendency one recognizes, consider having a conversation about it with a trusted friend. Or, depending on the relationship, one may think about asking the boss. The irony is in almost all these situations what we are concerned about exposing, has already been discovered by the boss and others. So, genuinely addressing the situation and demonstrating an effort to make an adjustment represents a maturity and most often brings increased credit rather than something negative.

Along with our management traits, we should also be clear about which management skills have firmly in our own toolbox. Be clear about your inventory of techniques and approaches that can be relied and is are used to solve problems. Consider brushing up in some way on what would strengthen our performance.

ESTABLISH A POSITIVE LEADERSHIP PROFILE

I define leadership profile broadly as the recognition a leader enjoys regarding the credibility, style, and overall effectiveness. For example, a leader who is forward thinking, high quality oriented, and has a history of resolving problems effectively and in a timely manner will be recognized by colleagues, upper management, and employees as having high management profile. One of the benefits of being recognized in this way is the boss and senior management are more likely provide the support that may be needed at various times. Other benefits include a greater likeliness of cooperation from colleagues throughout the organization when trying to solve inter-department operations issues. Being recognized in this way helps to smooth the inevitable bumps that occur which may otherwise be more difficult to manage.

A Strong Management Profile

- Set high performance and operations standards and expectations for one's self.
- Set standards that have a clear link to the organizations mission, objectives, and culture.
- Help managers establish clear thresholds for performance standards for his / management team and provides support to achieve those standards through sound coaching and mentoring practices.
- Is an effective communicator and able to elicit support from others to meet reasonable objectives?
- Works effectively with HR representatives.
- Works with and helps managers to achieve specific objectives in their departments.
- Is self-confident and has a good sense of when to lead and when to follow.
- Is recognized for being credible and trustworthy

Separating the Rough from the Diamonds

Eventually, managers who cannot meet performance standards need to be dismissed. The process is unpleasant, but not doing most often leads to more difficult circumstances. Avoiding this uncomfortable procedure has the effect of decreasing the net competency and strength of the management team. It reduces the management team's performance profile as a whole and can diminish operations efficiencies. In many cases not doing to diminishes employee morale. It needs to be accomplished with sensitivity and based on an undeniable and sufficient number of circumstances that demonstrates substantial deficiencies that resulted in personnel and or operational problems. Leaders need to work with the appropriate representative in HR to be sure the documentation reason for taking this action can't be denied or successfully challenged.

KEEPING THE VISION ALIVE

By keeping the vision alive, I mean creating a work environment where employees recognize their manager's ongoing interest and efforts to make improvements whenever possible. Successful leaders are able to find ways to continuously tweak, modify, and put new life into day-to-day operations. Team leaders should encourage managers to develop new and interesting initiatives for their workgroups. Often making even minor adjustments can have a very worthwhile impact on employee morale. Doing this gives all involved a sense of progress even if only "little" things are happening. However, these little improvements and adjustments aggregate and over time help build a mindset that helps to keep employees in a positive frame of mind. It also creates opportunities to build pride and a culture that supports everyone's willingness to look for ways to improve. The central objectives are to create a workplace environment where looking for ways to improve occurs equally from bottom up [and] top down.

Organizations use posters and create clever phrases that can be seen throughout work areas, but employees can also be encouraged to create their own initiatives. I have seen employees create simple but very interesting workplace initiatives that were later recognized and adopted by employees in other departments. These [department] plans need to be closely aligned to and support the organization's overall initiative.

I have found one way to foster such an environment is for managers to set a few minutes aside during each staff meeting to discuss quality issues. The conversation can begin by asking employees something like - what employees may have observed since the last meeting, or recently, that supports – or is counter to providing high-quality services or products - or a positive work environment. Having a brief, informal discussion [while respecting the privacy of those who may be a part of those observations] is beneficial. Doing so generates discussions about real situations and encourages employees to discuss opportunities for making improvements. I remember an employee talking about how chairs in their waiting room should be rearranged. An employee watched a patient seated in a small waiting room where chairs were set so people where close by and facing each other directly. The employee's observation was this must make anyone sitting in those chairs uneasy and feeling the wait time is much longer than it actually is. After the meeting chairs were rearranged. This little adjustment was perceived to be an improvement by employees and one that helped to reinforce the general culture of the work group, even little things are important. It was a small thing, but it evoked the idea that [this] workgroup is one that takes pride in providing the best service possible. In the end it was that positive continuing idea toward making improvements whenever possible that becomes the most important element, rather than moving the chairs.

GUARD AGAINST THE STATUS QUO

I have observed an interesting and consistent characteristic with high-performing leaders. They become uneasy when operations seem to be functioning smoothly and they begin to feel especially uneasy when discussions with their managers signal a sense of "mission accomplished." They know with such a mindset operations can become relaxed, taken for granted, and the drive to improve begins to erodes. Their subconscious seems to tell them, the status quo today will be only a memory with tomorrow's competition. Tomorrow, the competition may be on to something better. These managers are the canaries in the mine, and they are consistently drawn to think about what can be done to keep moving forward. New art work on the walls. Fresh paint in a drab looking waiting area. For these managers, a more efficient method for handling paperwork, an updated recognition program, or looking at new objectives are always up for discussion and consideration.

I have had very fortunate experiences working with leaders who demonstrated these characteristic and because of their - canary in the mine perspective - their operations were consistently recognized to have the best practices. It may be interesting to point out that although a few of these individuals were very high energy type A and gregarious in natures, there were others who had a more laid-back persona, but their common drive to "keep the ball rolling" was undeniable.

Reward and Recognition

Everyone looks forward to recognition and successful team leaders look for ways to satisfy this element of our human nature. Formal recognition comes at specific times usually after a project has been completed successfully. Sometimes recognition comes with something tangible, a certificate, a plaque, or a gift. But informal recognition occurs randomly to show appreciation for smart, particularly insightful thinking, or simply when a sound decision was made. Genuine informal expressions of appreciation from leaders builds and sustains morale among their managers and that helps greatly to further establish a strong and positive work environment. It also helps to encourage ongoing positive individual effort. Leaders who can express these simple acts of recognition freely with a smile, a simple nod of the head, or even a genuine "thank you" sends a powerful and meaningful message to their managers. These simple genuine personal communications trigger a chemistry in humans that moves us to do well and continually look for ways to meet and exceed expectations. It also further cements a culture of excellence in the workplace. Establishing such a culture gives managers confidence to think about and try new initiatives. The reality is our human nature drives us to build confidence, and giving recognition large or small when warranted strengthens an individual's effort grows and meet new challenges.

Humor

Humor is an essential ingredient in providing strong leadership, not a luxury. Humor works to strengthen collegiality within a management group and among colleagues. Leaders can use humor in many ways. It can be used intelligently and appropriately to address various situations that would be more difficult to work through otherwise. It can relieve tension from various circumstances. It redirects energy by creating a momentary break [in the action] that works to clear air, and our heads. It can be used appropriately to put aside embarrassment regarding an errant or unsuccessful but genuine effort. The specifics of that outcome can be addressed later at a more appropriate time.

Leaders who have great difficulty mustering a "funny bone" may be fortunate enough to have a member of their group who's timing and sense of humor can be relied upon occasionally to find a little levity in a situation. Humor, however, should not be used as a vehicle for sarcasm or ridicule, especially toward someone, no matter how a leader may feel so enfranchised. I have been present when a leader used humor in this way and the results were always negative. The uneasy chuckles it evoked were always short lived while their destructive nature carried a much longer shelf life. Leaders who use sarcasm or dark humor routinely risk revealing more about themselves than the person or situation they have targeted.

DISARMING THE SACRED COW

Few things can be more discouraging to creating a cohesive and high-functioning management team or group of employees than sustaining the "sacred cow" member whose word is intended to carry disproportionate weight. This is especially true when in one way or another those individuals seem to assume it to be their role. Management teams almost always have members with unique training and specific skill sets such as finance, personnel, facilities, compliance, etc., Their points of view, council, and opinions need to take the lead in discussions that relate to their specific expertise. However, when others consistently move to dominate a topic of discussion, the leader needs to disarm their imagined influence. Group leaders can balance participation by making a point to ask or challenge others on the team for their thoughts on what is being discussed or propose alternate ideas for all to comment. Developing a culture where conversation at operations meetings and staff meetings are balanced leads to having everyone "in the game" and that encourages full and more creative participation.

CHAPTER SUMMARY

- ➢ Characteristics of a high functioning management team include:
  - o A clear and realistic view of operations and personnel management objectives
  - o A collegial environment that encourages open to two-way communication within the group and its leader
  - o A commitment to a high standard for performance

- ➢ Is a reliable sounding board to the group leader that focuses on realities of operations especially for decision making
  - o Serve as advocates of their employees

- ➢ Assures equity in the organization's overall practice and decision making
- ➢ Demonstrates a well-grounded management philosophy regarding personnel and operations management, and personal conduct
- ➢ Demonstrates good recognition practices
- ➢ Sets clearly defined performance expectations
- ➢ Understands and can manage individual strengths
- ➢ Recognizes and manages individual limitations appropriately
- ➢ Demonstrates on going coaching and mentoring practices
- ➢ Exercises judicial use of the notion, "The sin is not necessarily the errant initiative or failed outcome - instead it is not having a willingness to experience the effort or the ability to learn from it"
- ➢ Demonstrates an element of humor in management style
- ➢ Be wary of the notion "mission accomplished"

CHAPTER TWO

THE MULE AND THE PURCHASER

A man wished to purchase a mule, and agreed with its owner that he should try out the animal before he bought him. He took the mule home and put him in the straw-yard with his other mules, upon which the new animal left all the others and at once joined the one that was most idle and the greatest eater of them all. Seeing this, the man put a halter on him and led him back to his owner. On being asked how, in so short a time, he could have made a trial of him, he answered, "I do not need a trial; I know that he will be just the same as the one he chose for his companion."

A Man Is Known by the Company He Keeps

Practical Application

Successful leaders identify, attract, and hire managers and staff who can bring quality and character to their organization.

Case Study

After six months of effort at her new job, Ellen could demonstrate virtually no improvement in performance among her employees, or with the department's operations inefficiencies. She was genuinely puzzled about this because her previous fifteen years of management experience had been positive and successful. She also began to sense upper management was perhaps beginning to see her as part of the situation rather than being its principle change agent. It was clearly time for Ellen to reassess her approach, evaluate her performance and her managers, and with them, do a comprehensive evaluation of the operation.

Discussion

The "wellness" of an operation, even with the circumstances as Emily found them, are most often directly related to the competencies and character of its managers. All operations have difficulties from time to time but when the frequency moves from being an exception to predictable or not surprising its leader needs to be at the forefront of implementing effective corrective action. To accomplish this, it's important to have managers with strong management profiles. Blaming employees as we saw in Chapter one's case study is not the answer. There may be a few or even a click of "bad apples" in a work group but the situation didn't evolve on its own. Someone hired and allowed those apples to develop and influence operations. Even with the circumstances in the above case study, Emily was dealt a bad hand, but positive changes can be made with the worst scenarios.

Emily needed to take charge of the situation. She understood blaming the employees could not be principle part of the solution. The question was where to start. Fortunately, Emily's boss, Patrick understood the difficulties and Emily was able to have helpful discussions and guidance about her initial observations, and within a month an action plan began to form that both could agree upon.

Early in my management career I was fortunate enough to have a boss who had truly excellent coaching and mentoring skills. He hired me into a very similar situation. One day as I was talking to him about the difficulties and challenges in the department, he reached into his desk drawer. He got a stuffed monkey from the drawer and put it on the desk. I continued, and he reached a second time to get a small palm size stone and put it next to the monkey. He put his hand up slightly to stop me and said the following. "I'm not going to take this monkey off your back. It's yours to deal with, but I am going to do everything possible to move the rocks that are in your way." That simple comment was all I needed to understand, and I had no doubt from that point forward where I stood with him or what our roles were in the process. I never forgot the power and value of what he said. I began to understand very quickly from that brief coaching experience what management matrix was, and found his coaching philosophy to be one that I would apply diligently throughout my management career.

Fortunately, Emily's manager had a similar approach. He understood the first task for Emily is to make a thorough and accurate assessment that would lead her to seeing the actual cause and effect issues - and avoid reacting to the many symptoms of the scenario. Things happen for a reason. Solutions to virtually all management situations come from collecting information objectively about the operation, evaluating it objectively, and filtering them through a cause and effect assessment process. This may seem at first to be a time-consuming process but it is not. Clues to questions regarding cause and effect and sorting symptoms from root cause can be accomplished in relatively short time if done properly and with a reliable process or regimen. The sole objective in doing this is that it brings one to visualize the critical path[s] that will lead to the best possible solutions.

In this situation the problems were standing long before Emily's time and they involved a large enough group of employees that Emily and Patrick felt outside help was indicated. Fortunately, the organization's

HR department had formally trained counsellors who were available and happy to help, and Harriet was tapped to assist. The assessment began with Harriet meeting with employees to get their views on the various problems they saw in the workplace. As can be expected, the conversation began with a few employees pointing to management as the central problem. Several charges were leveled at Emily which included things like she was not distributing the work fairly. Other complaints were about Emily being too harsh and even arbitrary when counselling or disciplining employees. There were several more general complaints about her allowing the work area to be cluttered and disorganized. They said established procedures were not consistently followed and employees had varying skill levels which caused work to be distributed unevenly. But predictably, other employees supported Emily as a hard working well intended manager who was overloaded with her own duties. Here is a summary of employee complaints.

1. Employees felt their work area was disorganized. Supplies, procedure books etc. were often not available when needed.
2. Procedures for specific tasks were not clearly defined in operating manuals so employees used their best guess at times to fill the void, which created inconsistencies in how tasks were completed.
3. Sometimes procedures were added with little or no notice which complicated work flow.
4. Employees' skill levels varied which lead to an uneven distribution of work.
5. Scheduling employees for weekend coverage seemed unfair at times.
6. Employees felt their supervisors were not as willing to help with procedures when staffing was short.
7. As for Emily, her frustration came from dealing with the various employee clicks and with individuals who exhibited passive aggressive conduct. She was also concerned about her own workload.

After Harriet and Emily reviewed the notes from the employee meeting. Emily expressed her frustrations with her workload. She also described the workgroup of approximately 70 FTEs had [clicks] of employees who seemed to be more interested in challenging efforts to improve operations than helping. Along with the clicks, Emily described a few employees who were particularly troublesome and who's primary mission seemed to be as passive aggressive as possible. A follow up meeting with the employees was scheduled. This time, both Harriet and Emily discussed specific issues Emily had with the employees. These observations were not vigorously challenged by the employees.

Harriet also talked with the supervisors who reported to Emily. They talked about the positive and not so positive things that were happening in the department. They saw most of the department's issues in the same way as Emily. The third meeting was with Harriet and Emily. Both Emily and Harriet summarized their discussions with employees and with Emily's managers.

We often hear that it is the little things that get the greatest response from employees, and this situation is a clear example of that general observation. Their problems evolved slowly over an extended period of time so they were difficult to see. However, after reaching a critical threshold with a relatively minor incident, it triggers a reaction where everything seemed to be going wrong at the same time. Operations and personnel problems do evolve slowly so it is sometimes difficult for managers to see the evolution and realize their operation is approaching a critical point. In many instances the "slow burn" occurs because employees and or managers make minor compensations without realizing it until they arrogate a much bigger problem. Let's look deeper into these little things in order to see how they can be avoided.

TWO KEY DIMENSIONS OF MANAGEMENT

Range of Accountability
and
Threshold for Taking Action

Managers have a wide range of responsibilities. Because of the many routine tasks, we perform in addition to what often seems to be a continuous parade of interruptions and new challenges, we prioritize various pieces of our jobs into a higher or lower priority. And we do this with good intensions about "getting to" the lower priority items - before the week or month is out. It's a common survival technique that helps us get through the day. The problem, of course, is this kind of prioritizing along with those good intensions impacts the operation in ways we sometimes don't realize. And doing so often contributes to employee morale issues because by the end of the week [or month] other new things occur and we lose sight of those "little things". This leads employees thinking their manager is not in touch with reality because their issues are not being addressed.

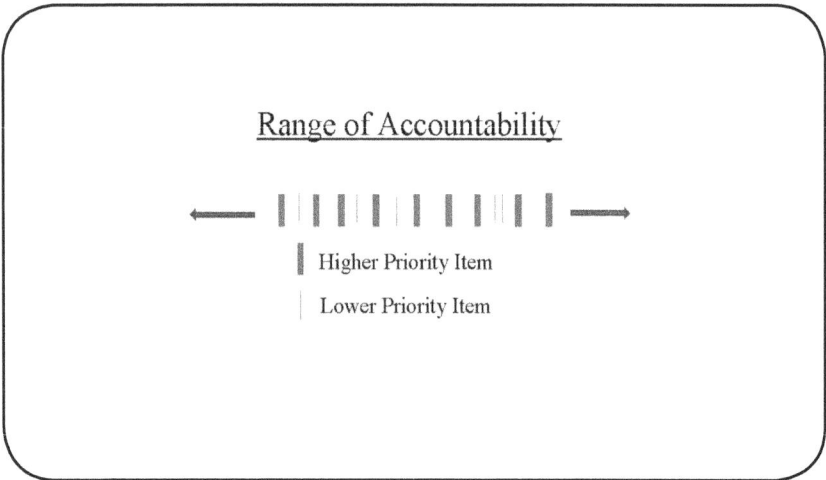

Range of Accountability

| Higher Priority Item

| Lower Priority Item

To get a better handle on this, it might be interesting for a manager to ask employees during a staff meeting what is it they "grind" about while on their way home from work or start thinking about while on their way to work. The answers could be surprising. This brings me to those two key dimensions of management.

Scope of Accountability refers to all those pieces of the operation's puzzle that influence everyday operations – and are very much in the manager's sphere of accountability and certainly include those low priority items. Let's consider a few very simple examples for a moment.

- Availability of supplies, equipment, and other items that staff depend on to do their jobs efficiently. [how often do employees complain about… this or that item is not where it needs to be]
- Fairness and consistently applied to operating regimens, such as a well-defined instruction for completing tasks and workflow.
- A balanced and fair staff coverage plan for maintaining operations
- Cleanliness and orderliness of the workplace
- Attention given to employee training, along with clearly defined competency standards for both employees
- Attention given to employee recognition and morale
- Quickness and appropriateness with which corrective action on a wide range of circumstances

It is not surprising how many of these [low priority] items Emily's employees complained about. As simple as these pieces of the operation may be individually, in aggregate they create a critical mass of issues that can have real influence on overall efficiency, errors, and certainly employee morale and cooperation. I can't tell you how many staff meetings I monitored over the years I heard employees complain about their managers who seem to overlook these simple items. And, in many cases their managers being completely puzzled about their employee's "random" complaints – sometimes expressing these complaints as "just whining". Sometimes managers and supervisors simply don't see these as real problems. They have bigger fish to fry, but employees deal with these issues several times an hour throughout the day - every day. The point is busy managers unwittingly take action on what they see as important and put other things outside their [real] scope of accountability to at a later time. For managers, handling [everything] and [perfectly] becomes an incredibly daunting and virtually impossible task. However, there are solutions to this dilemma that I will address later in the chapter. For the moment lets recognize the first dimension, Range of Accountability, and it impacts operations.

The second dimension of management I refer to is the threshold managers set for taking corrective action. In other words, at what level of personnel conduct or system dysfunction triggers managers to take corrective action. As we go through our daily management routines and make general observations about what is happening in the workplace, we see variances from the ideal, and often without realizing it, we decide to take action today or take corrective action at a more convenient time. The second dimension also takes into account the amount of latitude managers are willing to give before taking corrective action. Something may occur that is so far outside the established standard there is no question action needs to be taken promptly. However, there are many other occasions that are less so, when managers allow the circumstance more latitude than may be warranted before taking corrective action.

Recognizing one's threshold for taking action with various situations is an important element of management. Often managers and supervisors are not entirely aware of their trigger for taking action. We allow slippage, or simply lose track of the number of things that are functioning just a little outside of best practice. It is a concept we don't usually view. There was a brief discussion in Chapter One about the idea of managers knowing one self and this is an example of how that can apply. I can think of many situations where the department or workgroup manager felt confident about how they are handling scope and threshold when the reality indicated otherwise.

Threshold for Taking Corrective Action

Let's look at simple bar graph. People simply do not function perfectly all the time regarding every established standard and managers can't take action every time a minor variance occurs. But at some point, whether it is because of the degree or frequency of conduct or performance, managers need to act. Some managers are recognized to be more relaxed and tolerant while others are less so. The point is we should occasionally make a realistic assessment of variances regarding conduct and performance versus action taken or not taken, thinking about the following.

- What is my general tolerance and threshold level for taking corrective action?
- Is corrective action taken consistently regarding performance and conduct.
- Does corrective action I take on the same issue vary widely depending on the individual involved or and circumstances?
- How timely is corrective action taken after broaching the threshold?

When reasonable thresholds are set for various performance and conduct issues and acted upon in a timely manner;

- It creates a standard of quality from personnel and helps to assure high quality of services are provided
- It establishes predictability in the workplace. Employees like having clear and consistent criteria in the workplace. It provides a measure of safety for them to function.

Let's think about available to time for doing [everything to perfection]. Managers and supervisors can help themselves with the [Range of Accountability]. In some situations' managers have opportunities to delegate some of these tasks to individuals or to a separate team of employees. Keep in mind it's the employees who are most likely to benefit from having these items addressed so they are often willing to help improve their own work environment. Why not have them help? My experience is employees recognize these benefits and are willing to be part of the solution. For example, with the group of 70 employees in this case study the Emily was able to have 6 volunteers work on specific tasks that fell into the supervisor's low priority group of items. Two worked on updating and organizing two procedure books with guidance from their supervisor, and two were assigned to organize supplies in the work area. In this case, they worked directly with Emily and were also able to see where new and simple rules could be established to help keep the area organized. Two other employees agreed to manage the inventory and recommended a new system for ordering supplies which kept the store of inventory updated. They were able to see where specific supply items and instruments need to be placed for quick access. They were also able to establish new rules for other all employees to alert them or a supervisor when supplies are running low. Other seemingly small tasks were delegated to employees. Employees were given time during staff meetings to update everyone and felt the role they were playing and the recognition they got from everyone involved.

Everyone was happy to see progress toward making their areas an easier place to work and complaints about Emily subsided. Not all of Emily's problems were resolved with this, but it created a different and better environment that made it much easier for Emily and her supervisors to manage.

Three Critical Leadership Traits

Chapter one outlines the need for building a strong management team. In this chapter I want to discuss more specific elements of individual manager performance and begin with a discussion about three personal traits that I believe are among the most critical. I realize there may be a danger in reducing a topic as broad and complex as leadership traits into a simple bite-size package of three items. Yet, an absence of any one of these three traits will have a significant impact on the long-term success as a leader.

The three traits I'm referring to are: intellect, wisdom, and understanding. It seems we most often equate intelligence with simply being "smart". Webster describes intelligence as "the ability to learn or understand or to deal with new or trying situations." Webster also says; "The ability to apply knowledge to manipulate one's environment or to think abstractly......." These two explanations apply very well to what I refer to as management acumen. These also fit into management situations very nicely because assessing, dealing with circumstances, and manipulating [managing] operations issues are primary expectations of management. With all of this in mind, intellect, wisdom, and understanding also drives critical thinking processes when selecting management candidates for open positions.

Intellect within the context of this discussion is the ability to clearly think through a maze of distractions in work environment situations in order to recognize the essential pieces of [cause] versus [symptoms] that ultimately lead one to the best possible decision or action. It also helps managers consider more than one possible solution. Staying at the surface of a problem by focusing on its symptoms is convenient and tantalizing, but it can also be misleading and ineffective. Under the best scenario, it shows immediate gains but, in most cases, not long-term solutions. The capacity of a manager to make timely and insightful assessments, understand root cause, visualize different solutions, and then determine a critical path to the best possible solution are all strong indicators of management intellect, and a strong management acumen.

- Exercising wisdom is the second critical trait. Wisdom here is the ability to choose wisely and the best among the various possibilities for solutions or actions that may be considered. It drives managers to visualize the critical path to the best possible outcome. Developing and exercising one's wisdom will help a manager choose the best of the possible action plans from other choices that are being considered. Wisdom to a large degree comes from experience gained from observing outcomes and learning from past experiences. Its one reason why I talked earlier about leaders of management groups judiciously allowing their managers to exercise their own problem-solving abilities. Leaders need to appropriately and with a degree of sensitivity and caution, work with their managers to exercise their leadership. *"The sin is not necessarily the errant initiative or failed outcome – instead it is not having a willingness to experience the effort or the ability to learn from it"*

Wisdom also comes from what I addressed in Chapter One about knowing one's self. Recognize limitations - and take time to seek assistance from a trusted source. A measure of wisdom can be gained over time from open conversations with colleagues who have demonstrated their ability to consistently find solutions to challenging circumstances. Wisdom also grows when learning from recognizing when to lead and when to follow.

The third critical trait is an ability to demonstrate understanding. In this context I refer to understanding as being able to clearly see and appreciate the outcome and the likely impact decisions and actions may have on employees, operations, and depending on the circumstances - colleagues. Exercising a reasonable degree of [understanding] while considering various action steps is not being soft. It's being smart. Decisions need to be made with a clear appreciation of the impact on those involved. This is best accomplished by communicating before a decision is finalized with those who may be affected by an action or decision. Taking the opportunity to validate helps managers anticipate and gauge various outcome scenarios in advance of implementation. Which once again, is not being soft... doing so allows managers to consider ways the impact can be mediated which ultimately works to increase chances of success. Demonstrating a genuine understanding can build alliances and give colleagues an opportunity to react beforehand. Those colleagues are likely to remember your consideration, when their help may be needed another time to provide needed support.

SELECTING LEADERS

The fable in this chapter raises the question about the filtering criteria we have use to make the final candidate selection. Which characteristics and traits do we feel are most important? Although there are many to consider, the three I described above should be included. Certainly, depending on the specific vacancy, any one of these may be given a slightly higher or less so priority but the threshold for each should be high. The accuracy of prioritizing these to satisfy the best [fit] would certainly be a measure of the hiring manager's capability to fill key positions in the organization.

There are various ways hiring managers can assess their own criteria. Here are a few of my own. The first is to understand the candidate's thinking processes. How does he / she tend to react to various circumstances? Are they pragmatic? What is their baseline strategy when dealing with personnel or operations issues? Are they detail oriented? Do they mainly think analytically or by intuition? I certainly want to know if the candidate thinks logically. So, I'll give a slightly difficult personnel or operations management situation that needs to be solved. If the candidate begins by focusing only on the symptoms I described and then continues to describe action steps, I become concerned. I'm not looking for solutions to symptoms, I want to know about the root cause. In contrast to this if a candidate talks about the symptoms as I described them and then suggests a few possible underlying causes, I am more interested. On the other hand, if a candidate's conversation seems to meander between symptoms and root cause without a semblance of fact finding and decision-making regimen I'm turned off.

If I create a budget preparation situation for the coming year and ask the candidate to describe how he / she prepares for coming year's budget. If the candidate immediately talks about ways to reduce expenses – a yellow flag goes up once again. That may be part of the answer but I want to know if any notes are taken during meetings the current year. Meetings occur routinely with other department heads and senior management where changes in policy, process, new programs, and new regulatory requirements are discussed. Some of those situations can change or create new demands on my equipment and personnel for the following year and need to be accounted for when developing next year's budget. Those changes mentioned during meetings and random conversations need to be noted, filed, and used as references when preparing the new year's budget. Doing so will go a long way to help write and defend a more realistic budget for the coming year. A candidate who can talk to me about a file he or she keeps or some other technique that shows forethought gets my immediate attention. This is evidence that the candidate thinks clearly, is organized, and forward thinking. All are essential management elements.

The next line of questions I use relates to the candidate's understanding of human nature. Why human nature? Because the elements of human nature that are firmly and uniformly embedded in all of us [employees, the boss, senior management, colleagues] sets virtually all the ground rules for how people act. The candidate my not be thinking in terms of "human nature" but I want to know what [things] he or she feels are important when working with employees and colleagues. Using various scenarios like these to gauge management candidates thinking process is an important interviewing technique.

Human Nature, Exercising Power in Leadership

We have been talking about how important it is to motivate and engage employees by exercising various leadership styles and techniques. At seminars we commonly hear different versions of the idea "people first" but I haven't heard about employee management discussed in the context of human nature and the expectations that are embedded in all of our human nature. Employees are our most important and expensive resource and asset. We also hear that high morale among employees is vital to a smooth-running cost-efficient workplace and less management stress. I believe when managers think in terms of human nature and understand its impact on operations - opportunities for success increase many times over.

Recognizing how human nature impacts management is important because human nature drives virtually all employee behavior. Managers at all levels who recognize and use this reality to their advantage prove to be highly successful leaders. Here are a few points about knowing the [nature] of human nature that works to our advantage as managers. 1st, the same elements of human nature lay equally within all our employees [and] within all of us as managers; 2nd those elements of our human nature drive specific expectations; 3rd, they need be recognized and satisfied in reasonable and realistic fashion; 4th, those basic expectations are consistent and haven't changed over the past several thousand years. All of this is good news because its predictability makes it easier to manage.

MANAGERS ARE FROM MARS AND
EMPLOYEES ARE FROM VENUS

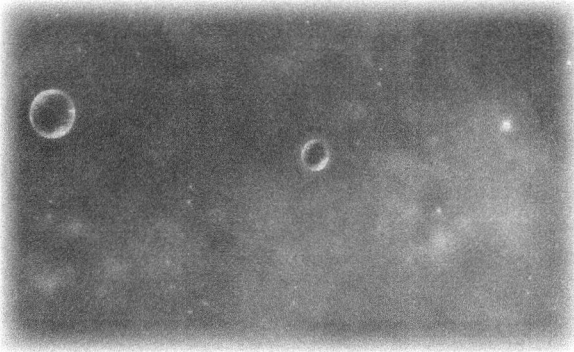

Organizations' as well have a nature of their own, and the key elements are embedded equally in all organizations, and if we think about this for another minute, we can see that an organization's [nature] also has its own set of expectations. An organizations' expectations appear in the form of mission statements, a vision, goals, objectives, policies, and procedures. These lead an organization to establish expectations that come alive through its management team.

The challenge to management is there is an inherent conflict with the expectations of an organization's [nature] and those of our employees' human nature. Let's take one example. One of our human nature elements that drives us is to be creative and function as individuals with a strong element for freedom and having control of our environment. But, the nature of an organization, through its policies and managers' is to be dominant and in control. All of this creates a kind of pressure of will among employees and their managers. A pressure that if not understood and managed well, can come to life as HR issues and operations inefficiencies. This one example helps to show why intellect, wisdom, and understanding are important traits for a manager to exercise. Successful management comes from smart manipulation of these elements. It helps us to define cause and effect and leads us to making the best possible choices for taking action.

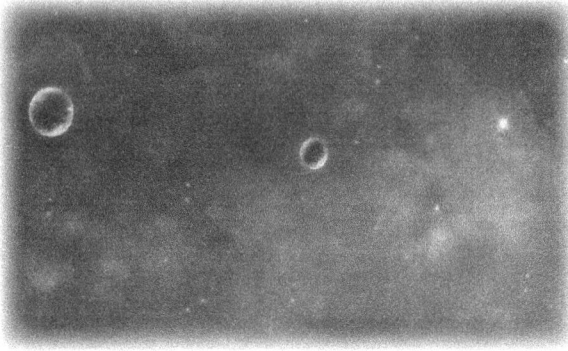

An interesting book was written several years ago about relationships among men and women. Its title is; <u>Men Are from Mars, Women Are from Venus: The Classic Guide to Understanding the Opposite Sex</u> In it, women were characterized by being from the planet Venus while men were proposed to be from Mars. The point of the book as I understand it is [with those two planets of origin] women have a different set of criteria for meeting their expectations while men, coming from an entirely different environment, have an alternate set of criteria. The authors say it is these different criteria along with their associated expectations that become the root of many of the relationship misunderstandings and problems among men and women. The book also goes on to suggest ways these differences can be addressed and successfully navigated.

Expectations of an Organization

Expectations of our Human Nature

- Generate A Margin / Profit
- Establish Policies and Procedures
- Demands Compliance
- Relies On Establishing and Maintaining Control
- Establishes Structure and Order

- Preserve A Measure of Individual Identification and Recognition
- Exercise A measure of Independence
- Exercise A Measure of Individual Creativity
- Be A Valued and Recognized As A Contributor
- Has A Strong Desire to be Apart of Something

We can make a similar analogy with management and employees with their opposing set of expectations. Here we see two sets of perfectly defendable expectations as well as the potential for disharmony. The point of this is not to assign labels but to appreciate the opposing set of legitimate expectations that leaders need to successfully navigate in order to keep this relationship healthy. I want to be clear with this explanation that when I encourage understanding and meeting employee expectations, I am not encouraging pandering or being [soft], or minimizing an organization's needs to survive and grow... it is being smart about how those needs are satisfied. Being fair, reasonable, while expecting high quality performance are not contradictory to being understanding and recognizing employees' reasonable expectations. Basic employee expectations that are defined by our nature need to be satisfied in a reasonable and appropriate fashion. Fortunately, there are relatively easy things managers can do to successfully navigate what may seem to be a full-blown conundrum.

FINDING AND HIRING DIAMONDS IN THE ROUGH

When considering applications for management positions I don't want to overlook those "diamonds in the rough" who populate virtually every organization. Once found, they can become a most valuable asset to an organization. I had a few opportunities to find these individuals during my management career, but one in particular comes to mind. Without going into the details, this employee was a part timer who was on the job only six months and worked a late weekend shift in a large and busy department. Her name came as a casual comment from a coworker during one of my rounds. I took the bait and later asked for the employee to stop by and talk for a few minutes. We talked briefly and I asked her to tell me a little about how in general terms she would describe her workplace environment as I used some of my filtering techniques as described above. The conversation broadened and I began to recognize some of the traits I know to be crucial. We began talking more specifically about one or two of the situation's employees were experiencing at the time and as the conversation continued, I realized I was checking off virtually all of the key traits.

After a few days of interviewing other outside very capable candidates I thought more seriously about this individual. The only additional feedback I got was that she was well liked. I was feeling uneasy about her taking on the responsibility of successfully managing more than 100 people in a very active and diverse work environment. But I also felt I had to trust my instincts. I talked with my boss about the risks of hiring this neophyte candidate but he agreed I should make the offer. The decision turned out to be one of best personnel decisions I ever made.

She proved to have the traits and characteristic the situation needed. She was very coachable and within six months the department was moving in the right direction. This is an unusual situation in the context of finding a diamond in the rough, but it makes a strong point that candidates who possess key traits as outlined above provide great potential for success no matter their current situation. The following months progress exceeded my expectations. The candidate was able to demonstrate how mentally confident she was which allowed her to provide a reasonable degree of flexibility for her employees without losing control or threatening the departments objectives. In this case the remaining pieces to hiring such a diamond in the rough was proving continued coaching and mentoring as was indicated.

EVALUATING CANDIDATES FOR SUPERVISORY AND MANAGEMENT POSITIONS

1. Basic information.
   a. Type of facility, organization, or circumstance where the candidate is currently employed
   b. How long manager has been in the position
   c. How many people does a manager oversee
   d. Type of services the manager's workgroup provide
   e. Does the manager – manage other managers or employees
   f. Current operating budgeting responsibilities, successes and failures
2. What are two important things [the candidate] learned about leading employees?

3. How do you manage stress?

4. What would the candidate say are two important things that lead to employee and manager disconnects?

5. Would you discuss one or two examples of what managers can do to build a workplace environment where employee morale and quality of service or product is high?

6. How important do you think it is for a manager to develop a workplace environment where employees are engaged in their work?
   a. How does employee morale impact customer [patient] services they provide?

7. I would like to ask a few questions about working relationship between a manager and his / her boss.
   a. What kind of things can manager and his/her boss do that would help build a positive working relationship?

8. Would you talk with me about an operations or personnel problem you had to resolve?
   a. How did you research the situation?
   b. What needed to be corrected and how did you decide what it was?
   Look for how the candidate's approach fits the organization and would help support the vision and objectives of the organization.

9. Ask the candidate to talk about key accomplishments and why they were important.

10. Ask the candidate about management philosophy and the approach he/she uses to manage operations and personnel.

11. What does the candidate feel are most important with when communicating with employees and colleagues.

12. Ask the candidate about how employees' work can be aligned with the organization's vision and mission.

13. Determine how much mentoring or training the candidate may need. Consider personality fit with other managers and senior management.

CHAPTER SUMMARY

➢ Department managers and supervisors need to have a realistic vision of their;
   o Management style
   o Philosophy regarding personnel management
   o Criteria for valuing employees

➢ Work effectively with the Two Dimensions of Management
   o Range of Accountability
   o Threshold for Taking Action
      ▪ Demonstrate success with delegating tasks to employees

➢ Recognize and work effectively to balance the organization's expectations and those embedded in our human nature
➢ Appreciate and recognize the candidate's thinking processes and evaluate them carefully as well as their technical skills.
   o Depending on the scope of the candidates' current responsibilities, technical skills may not <u>always be the only</u> or most important criteria

➢ Watch for and evaluate [in house] talent for management positions
➢ Develop a defined process with specific criteria that need to be satisfied when interviewing candidates for management positions
   o Watch for three key traits; Intellect, Wisdom, Understanding.

➢ Managers are responsible for establishing clearly defined standards for employee skills and competencies, instituting effective assessment tools, establishing ongoing training, and exercising appropriate and effective discipline when indicated.

CHAPTER THREE

THE MAN, THE BOY, AND THE DONKEY

A Man and his son were once going with their Donkey to market. As they were walking along by its side a countryman passed them and said: "You fools, what is a Donkey for but to ride upon?"

So the Man put the Boy on the Donkey and they went on their way. But soon they passed a group of men, one of whom said: "See that lazy youngster, he lets his father walk while he rides."

So the Man ordered his Boy to get off, and got on himself. But they hadn't gone far when they passed two women, one of whom said to the other: "Shame on that lazy lout to let his poor little son trudge along."

Well, the Man didn't know what to do, but at last he took his Boy up before him on the Donkey. By this time they had come to the town, and the passers-by began to jeer and point at them. The Man stopped and asked what they were scoffing at. The men said: "Aren't you ashamed of yourself for overloading that poor donkey of you and your hulking son?"

The Man and Boy got off and tried to think what to do. They thought and they thought, till at last they cut down a pole, tied the donkey's feet to it, and raised the pole and the donkey to their shoulders. They went along amid the laughter of all who met them till they came to Market Bridge, when the Donkey, getting one of his feet loose, kicked out and caused the Boy to drop his end of the pole. In the struggle the Donkey fell over the bridge, and his fore-feet being tied together he was drowned.

Please all, and you will please none.

PRACTICAL APPLICATION

Trying to please all results in exercising little authority for making decisions.

CASE STUDY

Joan has been managing her work group for several years. She is a friendly person and a solid manager who is interested in providing high-quality customer services. She trains her staff effectively and uses sound judgment to direct operations and provides support where needed. However, new demands on services resulted in the need for a new work schedule. To this point, the workgroup had been able to close their area for lunch for forty-five minutes and enjoy having lunch together, however, the growth of the service outpaced this practice. Also, additional coverage hours were needed, because the workload on the evening and weekend shifts increased. Additional staff were hired to work the new weekend slots. The long-standing and highly valued lunch schedule had to be abandoned along and a new rotation for staffing caused controversy among Joan's employees, and she had to make hard decisions.

The more senior employees felt strongly they should have priority. It was their effort, time, and competencies that helped bring the department to the current level of success. But, the less senior people felt their individual roles and responsibilities contributed equally to the services the department provides, and they must be counted on to contribute equally with the senior employees to achieve future successes. The newer employees felt favoring senior people was unfair. Both senior and newer employees had worked well together up to this time; however, the new situation became contentious, and Joan felt more and more pressure to make decisions and resolve the situation. Joan was at a loss to reconcile and make a decision for fear of angering and losing the support and loyalty of the senior group and a few of who she considered to be key high-performing long-time employees she had come to depend on.

DISCUSSION

Trying to please all, a group, or an individual can lead to very difficult decision making and complications. Attempts to resolve conflicts among employees can have an unexpected effect on employees in the workgroup. These situations are laden with traps of all sorts and because of this, Joan delayed decision making which only increased anticipation and actually lead to new complications. Making no decision within a reasonable period of time can be perceived as the decision. There are no hard-and-fast rules that provide answers for exactly how these conflicts can be resolved, but perhaps a few points can be defined and used as a reference with these situations.

Despite how uncomfortable it may be, seeking help through open discussions with employees about reasonable alternatives can give clues for possible solutions. Sometimes the air is thick in these situations so the first task is for managers to maintain control by refocusing the objective from people to specific issues. Asking employees for and considering suggestions is not a retreat from management's responsibility. Allowing employees to openly discuss their concerns and help solve problems can create a stronger workplace environment where openness is viewed as a strength rather than a challenge to authority. Being open to employees' suggestions does not signal managerial weakness. This is true especially in situations where there may be various alternatives or latitude for resolution. It shows a manager's willingness to be flexible and a measured with decision making. Caution is advisable as well. I have seen managers become too willing to find answers by yielding to pressure from employees. I have also seen when making the easier answer actually frustrated employees. One way to avoid these problems is for Joan to be clear with a discussion about where the boundary lines are for an acceptable solution lay, and have reasons for where those boundaries must hold.

The organization's basic needs must be met, but all possible considerations need to be heard. It also helps to recognize with employees that there are no perfect answers or silver bullets that will solve their problem. Exercising intellect, wisdom, and understanding is the best way to find solutions. Fortunately, most often when employees suggest possible solutions to personnel or operations, they advocate a very realistic – even a conservative point of view. Decision makers should, when it is appropriate, consider the knowledge pool among employees who live the details of their jobs. They can provide insight that may not be apparent to management. They tend to suggest solutions that are acceptable because they fully realize how a too generous or creative solution could impact them. Certainly, getting employees involved in problem solving may not be appropriate in all situations, but when managers see the possibility, it can be used to a manager's advantage. The point here is decision making, especially for contentious and difficult circumstances, can be lonely at times but the processes doesn't always have to be a lonely one.

A critical element for management when working through conflict resolution situations is to keep communication with employees open and honest. A manager might say… I want to be flexible but I don't want to loss control or threaten the product or services we provide in any way. It's a manager's core responsibility to protect the boundaries best practice. Employees may not like what they are hearing but the majority will at least recognize and appreciate the honesty and the rationale reasonable and well-defined boundaries. Open and honest communication also helps to keep employees from editorializing and putting their own spin on the situation. Doing so also discourages erroneous and self-serving employee interpretations. Talking with employees one on one can sometimes lead to important insights but in these situations be careful about being miss quoted.

Being Alert to Problems

Having managed more than a few conflict scenarios I have come to understand it's the mindset of the supervisor or manager that often determines how discussions with employees occur and ultimately what decisions are formed. I have seen decision makers approach similar conflict situations with different mindsets and have very different outcomes. Managers who viewed their employees as being difficult to work with no matter the effort, versus managers who begin the process by anticipating the best from employees will most likely see their predictions come true. There are degrees of difference with these possible outcomes, of course, but on balance the outcome is heavily dependent on the manager's attitude and assumptions going into these situations. These mindsets will lead one to exhibit not so subtle signals with things like tone of voice, body language, and word choices that signal employees to "get ready" and prepare for giving a complimentary reaction. It means managers would do well to get their emotions and apprehensions under control and demonstrate a respect for employees' points of view and approach the situation with the best possible mindset.

Time should be made before the final decision to validate or discard points of view that have no place for consideration. Arguing these issues during a meeting with employees is only distracting and accomplishes very little. A key objective is to get everyone or at least as many as possible thinking about the reality of cause and effect of the issue in the same way, so the final management decision will at least be properly targeted. A durable decision needs to satisfy three basic criteria; have the facts accurately in mind, make an accurate assessment of the facts, and the decision properly targeted on the interpretation. The resulting action or decision will most likely be able to stand up well to objective scrutiny and the test of time.

I want to use an abstract example to help make a point about conflict resolution. Let's use the example of driving a car. We learned and prepared with coaching and our first few driving experiences how to navigate various situations. We learned how to apply the brakes. When to apply them and how firmly or softly. We learned how to gauge safe distances while traveling at certain speeds. We learned the rules of the road etc., etc. We learned and prepared ourselves so well that these lessons have become "internalized" to the degree we don't think specifically about them as we approach various situations. We don't think specifically about moving our foot from the floor to the accelerator or brake or moving our hands to the steering wheel to turn the car to avoid an accident. We just do it.

The point I want to make with this example is that managers have similarly learned and prepared in various ways to handle management conflict situations. We learned from coaches, mentors, things we read, and our own observations and direct experiences. But what I have seen with conflict resolution is, we can lose sight of what was learned because of the complexity or the stress of circumstances we face. It may be the result of pressure for making a decision quickly, or the confusion that comes with extenuating circumstances we didn't expect, or perhaps the complications that are imposed by new situations we have no control over. All of these possible circumstances work to cloud those [best practices for decision making we learned] and we yield the emotions of the situation – trying to please. These can lead us to decisions that are premature and focused on the wrong pieces of the puzzle. And with this, we can lose sight of the basic criteria for a durable decision. We can avoid getting caught in these distracting elements by simply taking a little time to stop, think through how the problem evolved, understand root cause, and then sort through possibilities for resolution. In effect, we need to gauge our own mindset, recalibrate, and refocus. It may be helpful to consider the following.

Considerations before the decision is finalized.

- o Be sure something actually needs to be corrected, improved, or changed
    - Maybe small adjustments can make a worthwhile difference
- o Be clear about possible alternative solutions
- o Will additional resources be needed including new funding, personnel, equipment, supply items, etc.
- o Know the actual timeline for making a decision
- o Research and assess the circumstances and differentiate symptoms from root cause
- o How will the outcome be measured and evaluated
    - Are there specific way points that can visualized to help assure efforts to improve the situation are moving along as expected.
- o Evaluate the need for staff training
- o What upper management should know about the situation
- o Research and apply best practices where ever possible
- o Demonstrate an understanding about how the decision will impact all involved and make allowances where possible.
- o Hold firmly to reasonable and necessary boundaries for identifying acceptable solutions

I. Let's consider the employees for a minute and think about the information they should have about upcoming decision.

- o The purpose and benefits of the decision
- o The circumstances that triggered a need for a decision
- o The criteria for making the best possible decision

o The possibility of considering various solutions and what would be out of bounds

o Is there a need for training because of new procedures and or equipment

o Timeframe for decision making

o The purpose and value of the decision and its resulting action

o Considerations regarding how employee concerns can be balanced appropriately with the reality of operational needs.

o Employees need to recognize the commitment to implement the decision.

o The process for implementation needs to be as simple as possible with details regarding its key points such as timeframe and process, expectations of management, expectations of employees, etc.

o Employees should know how the success or benefits of the decision will be measured.

CHAPTER SUMMARY

➢ Decision making can be lonely at times, but the process that leads to a decision doesn't have to be lonely.

➢ The first criteria for reaching a decision is to satisfy the *needs of the operation*. Once those needs are defined the second criteria is to appropriately address the employee's basic expectations.

   o The expectations of building equity for employees.

   o Avoid favoring an individual [special] employee or a recognized group of employees.

   o Maintain two-way communication. Employees expect to be informed and kept up to date on where things stand and what they can expect.

➢ Review and objectively evaluate all suggestions regardless of the source.

   o Be aware of underlying motives of those suggesting alternatives. Consider the specifics of how a suggestion will support and improve quality of products & services.

➢ Preview the decision with managers and employees and get feedback.

➢ Communicate and implement the decision. Tell why alternatives solutions where are not acceptable.

   o Reinforce the need for compliance.

   o Be clear about your commitment to enforce the decision.

➢ Keep the boss up dated.

➢ Provide training if indicated.

CHAPTER FOUR

THE EAGLE AND ARROW

An Eagle was soaring through the air when suddenly it heard the whizz of an Arrow, and felt itself wounded to death. Slowly it fluttered down to the earth, with its life-blood pouring out of it. Looking down upon the Arrow with which it had been pierced, it found that the shaft of the Arrow had been feathered with one of its own plumes.

"Alas!" it cried, as it died: "We often give our enemies the means for our own destruction."

PRACTICAL APPLICATION

The manner and Skill we exercise with verbal communication will accelerate or limit our success in management.

CASE STUDY

David was asked to facilitate a work group to find solutions to a broad range of patient scheduling problems and inefficiencies that were occurring among several hospitals that are part of a healthcare system. David was chosen for this task because of his past experience with these activities at each of the facilities. Five other mangers were selected by senior management to be a part of the work group. Patients and treatment centers were frequently reporting the problems with scheduling patients. All members of the workgroup had strong management profiles and were very happy to be selected because their departments were experiencing these scheduling problems. At the first meeting David, with some difficulty, summarized senior management's expectations including acceptable parameters for recommended solutions, new resources senior management was willing to provide, and a timeline for the workgroup to present their findings and recommendations. A few minor points were missed that the managers felt were important. But other problems were apparent with David's summary and manner of delivery that evoked concern among the group. Although he understood the mechanics and complexities of patient scheduling, he was not able to express his ideas clearly. He tended to ramble when explaining his observations, and sometimes completely miss interpreted questions from the group. The second meeting ended with the group feeling their time has been wasted. After the third meeting with David, a new facilitator was selected.

DISCUSSION

There are two very basic pieces involved with verbal communication. Sending and receiving the message. Sounds simple, right. Not so fast, communicating effectively requires not only specific techniques but can be considered something of an art form which needs to be practiced. Think for a moment how much time on the job we actually spend sending and receiving messages. Think also about the impact these have on a manager - on the job successes. It should not be under estimated.

Effective communication gets things accomplished efficiently and builds a leader's credibility within the organization and among colleagues. Effective communication works to validate one's competencies all of which helps to secure one's standing in an organization and with employees.

Listening also requires a huge percentage of our time, and what we hear, interpret, and comprehend from what was actually said can determine the outcome of a single event, a project, or even a career. With verbal communication the person speaking has at least ½ the responsibility for how accurately a message is interpreted and comprehended. The speaker's responsibility lies with things like word selection, manner and tone of delivery, and body language. There are other elements the person speaking needs to accomplish, but these are primary and constant with all verbal communication. I will address the listener later in the chapter, but for now, the listener has roughly the other half of the responsibility with things like how accurately the message was heard, how successfully the listener stayed focused on the words that were used, avoided distractions, and accurately interpreted what was said. Most often when we speak, we assume all these key elements are occurring. If either the person speaking or listening do not meet their responsibilities adequately, the communication is likely to fail in some way. For those in leadership positions communicating effectively is not only a career sustaining tool, over time it can be a career survival tool.

When speaking we often take a lot for granted about what and how we speak, and how what we say is interpreted. Fortunately, we have many examples from people who have provided powerful and highly effective verbal communications that we can explore and reference. Four of those are listed below. Countless others can be found in our country's forefathers' speeches. I'm not advocating managers need to speak with such a degree of eloquence and power, but there are a few important constants we can derive from their examples that can help us become more effective communicators.

- John F Kennedy, President
- Ronald Regan, President

- Winston Churchill, Prime Minister Great Britain
- Walter Cronkite. CBS Anchor News Man

Speaking doesn't happen for its own sake. The point is building strong verbal skills has one purpose – to accomplish something – most often accomplish something for ourselves. Speaking well and effectively projects credibility and self-confidence that encourages listeners to – listen and comprehend. Our choice of words and manner of delivery can work to "hook" listeners to the message we want to convey and create a clear understanding of that message.

We can take important clues about effective verbal communication examples such as those of John Kennedy when he said "Don't ask what your country can do for you, ask what you can do for your country." Or when he said "We choose to go to the moon not because it is easy, but because it is hard." There are thousands of examples when speakers verbally created a [strong] mental image that works to connect us to their central message. Roosevelt talking about Pear Harbor, "A day of infamy" induced a sense of indescribable and calamity that called us to arms. Churchill about D day "We shall provide against, and thus prevail over the dangers and problems of the future, withhold no sacrifice, grudge no toil, seek no sordid gain, fear no foe" created a sense of unleased courage to withstand hardships. These show the central objective of verbal communication which is to create a mental image in the listener. A mental image in every day terms that may not be so dramatic – but believable and one that encourages listeners to focus on what we say and remember. Everyday communication will be more modest, but those of us in leadership positions need to create mental clear images with employees and colleagues with our verbal communication. The message and mental image we send at any given time may be a simple one, but no less important.

Below are four key benefits of practicing effective verbal communication techniques while in one-on-one situations, small group, or large group presentations.

- Improves Understanding
  - o Creates less opportunity for confusion and limits the opportunity for others to editorialize their version of the message.

- Improves Cooperation
  - o People are more likely to provide their support if they clearly understand the concept and the key details of the message

- Helps to Establish A Measure of Confidence
  - o A clearly stated, accurate, and appropriately delivered verbal communication builds confidence in those who receive the message.

- Builds Efficiencies
  - o The message is readily and quickly understood, requires less follow up and results in fewer errors through miss interpretation.

When we speak our verbal communication in virtually any situation builds a perception in others about who we are. It adds to our personal [bank] account with the organization's leaders as well as employees.

A Little Preparation is Always Indicated

When we are anticipating a conversation, it is wise to make some preparations. It's important to create a mental image of ourselves when communicating. Picture one's self speaking clearly and with confidence. Ideally that mental image should represent the confidence we feel with our choice of words, and the clarity of thought and the research we did to validate the message. Be clear about choice of words you may use and the manner in which you will verbalize the message. That mental image should include a posture [body language] that fits the situation. Prior to an important discussion it is helpful to prepare for a conversation by making a mental list of the key points that could make a difference to listeners rather than depend on them coming to mind randomly.

The more we think about and practice these things, they will become second nature. Such practice will also help us manage challenging conversations.

Body Language

As we create a positive mental image of ourselves while talking in virtually any setting, our body language automatically follows. Our body language [posture] forms automatically to what we are thinking. If the purpose of the communication is to motivate and create an energy in the room, the speaker's mental image will encourage the body to represent what the speaker is thinking and hopefully create a complimentary reaction from listeners. If the purpose of the communication is to deliver a more serious message the body will take a posture that signals the nature of that message. Our body language very often telegraphs what we are really thinking and the nature of the message. It also helps the audience to receive the message more clearly. We here suggestions that we should use good body language, but it's what we are thinking that most often drive our body language. For those listening, our physical being can be as much a part of the message as the words we use.

Here are a few additional points:

- Try to create a mental attitude that best fits the situation without pre judging the person or group listening.
- Use the available space wisely
  o In a small meeting room, if standing stay in a confined area at an appropriate distance from those listening
  o In a large lecture hall feel free to walk about in a larger but defined area
- In any space try to make eye contact occasionally with people around the room
- Maintain a professional posture without being stilted. To make an analogy, think business casual

I have found that it is helpful to assume the person our group of people we are speaking to are [who I would like them to be]. In other words, don't make assumptions about those who will be hearing the message. For example, don't assume the listener's willingness or unwillingness to accept what you are about to say, or make an assumption about their ability to comprehend the message. Don't take the bait and work on an assumption listener are going to be particularly negative or positive to what they hear. You may be accurate in that assumption, but don't telegraph it, doing so tends to accelerate the situation. Certainly, don't make the assumption the person or group does not have the mental capacity to understand the subtleties of what is to be said. Wait for questions to confirm one way or the other and respond respectfully.

Making these assumptions teases one into building a pre-strategy for the conversation or presentation which can be completely wrong. If a speaker assumes those listening will not be willing to accept what is to be presented, a speaker is likely to begin with a tone that is overly aggressive in order to overcome anticipated objectives. Or, a speaker may adopt a passive manner of delivery in order to avoid conflict that is anticipated. Either approach has the potential to antagonize the situation and once that environment is created, it can be difficult to redirect to a more neutral state. Assuming those listening do not have the capacity to understand the details of the communication may create a strategy that causes a speaker to over explain or talk down which is certain too infuriate those listening. Those listeners can quickly feel a speaker's assumption through body language and that will surely cause an unfavorable reaction.

Todd Smith[1] offers online 10 important communication skills that summarize very nicely the importance and art of effective verbal communication.

- Be friendly
    - o We are subconsciously drawn to people who are friendly because they make us feel good and bring more enjoyment to our lives.

---

[1] Verbal Communication Skills Worth Mastering / little things matter http://littlethingsmatter.com/blog

- Think Before You Speak
  - o Many people say whatever goes into their minds without putting a thought into what they are saying.... which ends up reflecting poorly on themselves.

- Be Clear
  - o Most of us don't have the time nor do we want to spend our emotional energy to figure out what someone else is trying to way. When there is something you want to say, ask yourself, what is the best way I can communicate the point....

- Don't Talk Too Much
  - o Very few people like to be around someone who talks to much and dominates the conversation.

- Be Your Authentic Self
  - o People are attracted to someone who speaks from the heart and is genuine, transparent, and real.

- Practice Humility
  - o Humility is having a modest view of one's own importance. People who speak with humility and genuine respect for others are almost always held in high regard.

- Speak with Confidence
  - o Speaking with confidence does not counter the need for humility. Speaking with confidence includes words you choose, the tone of your voice, your eye contact, and body language. These are supported by what you have validated and know to be correct.

- Focus on Body Language
  - o Body language communicates respect and interest in those listening. It gives real meaning to your words.

- Be Concise
  - o We become irritated when someone speaking can't get to the point. As yourself, how can I say what needs to be said in the fewest words possible while being courteous and respectful.

- Learn the Art of Listening
  - o Being an attentive listener is as important in verbal communications than any words that can come out of your mouth. Show sincere interest in what is being said, ask good questions, listen for the message within the message, and avoid interrupting.

CREATE A MENTAL IMAGE

Hopefully when communicating, the mouth is driven by the brain. Let's think for a moment about Olympic athletes and how this analogy can apply to verbal communication. We have heard sports commentators describe an Olympic athlete before, say making a ski run. The athlete is preparing with eyes closed for the run by using both the left and right sides of the brain to mentally visualize all the turns and related distances they will encounter against the anticipated speed while skiing down the mountain. Doing this helps them anticipate each turn, prepare, and navigate at seemly lightning speed. There's no time to think as the skier approaches each turn. Their moves have to be internalized to the point that they are executing without thought. A gymnast will pause and concentrate before performing a complex routine on the beam. These exercises become mental practice runs and this is an essential preparation for what's about to happen.

When we speak, we can also use our left and right brain to create mental images of us communicating effectively by creating a positive state of mind about what we want to say. The result is we can create a mental environment for ourselves that will help us deliver even difficult messages effectively and make a powerful presentation. The mental image we create for ourselves can be recognized by the audience's as confidence and believability.

The Art of Listening
What…. What did he say????

Humans do not have a very strong reputation for being excellent listeners. There are many reasons for occasions when we don't listen well. A game I remember playing as in the classroom called whispering down the alley provides interesting insight regarding this. In a classroom with about 15 young adults a very short simple message was given to the first person. By the time that sentence is sent, comprehended and, resent to the 15th persons, it can hardly be recognized. As adults, we deal with many distractions and urgencies that cause us to lose focus so we don't always hear accurately what was said. Here's a simple analogy. I have heard music played from a CD player when there were obvious flaws on the disc that caused skips and repeats. But when I played the same CD on my computer, the music sounded fine. The difference is that the computer has a digital process that "stitches" flawed areas of a disc and it "makes up sound" by using a sound averaging process. We do the same with the computers on our shoulders. Our mind can actually fill the gaps when we are distracted for a second or two, and at times it "tells" us what we think we should have heard rather than what was actually said. That sub-conscious process builds an [artificial – and wrong] message to substitute for what we missed. Sometimes our minds allow us to drift into another world altogether and day dream as we believe we are really listening. Maybe it's recalling a troublesome conversation we just had with someone. Or it may be about being sure to send in the mortgage payment tonight, and so on. All the while we believe we are listening to what is being said.

Like speaking, listening seems an easy thing to do, but to listen well takes an awareness and practice. Also, like speaking we can think about listening as an art that we should practice throughout the day, but it also requires specific skills. Too often we listen but don't hear and that causes us to miss a message altogether or miss interpret what was said.

Here are just a few conditions that cause this to happen.

- We hear something that strikes us a certain way and we immediately move to possible arguments about what was said and confuse what was said without mental arguments.

- Our minds immediately move to solving a problem that was presented and we block what was said afterward
- We don't agree with the information that was presented and we get upset or angry which sometimes allows us to miss interpret or discount the message
- Outside distractions may be competing with our ability to focus on the discussion
- Our minds drift to a personal issue we may be struggling with
- We consider the information boring and repetitive and mentally turn it off with the thought we know what he / she is saying.

The result of this aberrant listening can lead listeners to a variety of problems such as we;

- Don't actually hear or understand all of what was said
- Don't hear all of what was said - AND sometimes we mix our own thoughts at the time with those of the speaker. The result is our mind over rides and interprets sub consciously something different from what was actually said.

In order to get the full benefit of listening two different processes need to be exercised. One is how well we <u>manage</u> what we hear and the second is how accurately we interpret what we hear. For example, let's say we hear something with which we fully agree. We are pleased to hear what was said. How might that message be managed? Well, we might simply agree and walk away confident about the message. Or we may be so enthusiastic that the message is aligned with our own thoughts on the topic that we infer some of our own thoughts into what was actually said. The problem is, the speaker didn't actually say what we inferred. By not managing what we heard well, the speaker's message is blended with our thoughts and we end up miss interpreting. Sounds unlikely? How many times have we heard someone say, to a listener.... no, no that's not at all what I said. A listener's primary responsibility is not to agree or disagree, it is to comprehend and then get confirmation in some way if there is any doubt about the message. This is especially important to consider when the political environment is not positive.

Miss understanding or miss interpretation can also occur if a listener hears something he or she doesn't agree with. Here, a listener may feel angry or offended with what was said the listener almost immediately broadens the meaning of what was actually said beyond the speaker's words. There is a plethora of circumstances that can work against us when listening. One needs to be an active listener, but hearing the words alone isn't active listening. Listening carries with it the responsibility to not just hear but interpret the message accurately without truncating it or broadening. Be free to validate or qualify what was said. In some cases, the wrong choice of words is used and a different message is sent from what was intended. A listener may ask, "Did I hear you correctly when you said ....". Or, "Would you state that a little differently for me so I'm sure to understand". We don't generally think in terms of managing what we say and hear, but in fact that is exactly our responsibility when speaking and listening.

TIMES WHEN WE CAN'T LISTEN

There are other times at work or in our personal lives when we simply can't stop and listen carefully or have a conversation when someone asks. However, even this simple situation needs to be managed to avoid problems. When these situations occur, one needs to stop for a moment and make provisions to have the conversation at another time. Ask the person who wants the conversation to phone later, "Please make an appointment to talk", or "stop into my office later". Making sure we provide this option helps to both secure the conversation and extends common courtesy which the other person will appreciate.

CHAPTER SUMMARY

➢ Effective communication can influence one's career.
  ▪ Various techniques can be used while speaking to avoid distractions around us.
  ▪ When listening our minds take us to where our eyes are focused. When our eyes drift from someone speaking, we loss focus and will concentrate less on what is said.

➢ Some preparation is always needed even with casual conversation. This includes such things as;
  o Choice of words
  o Tone of speech
  o Appropriate body language
  o Formulating the central message
  o Be aware of one's mindset when anticipating a conversation.
    ▪ Feeling angry, distrustful, challenged, etc. before speaking will be recognized by those listening. Beginning a conversation with these emotions will distract a listener and create a difficult atmosphere for conversation.
  o Gauge the nature of the conversation in advance and select words, tone, and thoughts that best fit the circumstances.

➢ We should take advantage of the influence our brains provide by allowing us to visualize delivering a convincing and valid message
  o Build sentences that have logical and focused ideas
  o Create effective mental imagery in those listening that can help listeners absorb what is being said

➢ Active listening is more than hearing the words, it also requires verifying, managing, and accurately comprehending.

- o Take the opportunity to ask follow up questions of the person speaking to be sure the message heard is what the speaker <u>intended.</u>
- o Separate the person speaking from what is being said. A speaker's mannerisms and mode of speaking can be distracting and frustrating to a listener.
- o The basic purpose of listening is the have a full and accurate understanding of what is being said.

- ➤ When circumstances do not allow for an immediate conversation, provide an opportunity for discussion at another time.
- ➤ Practice preparing for formal and casual conversation with colleagues, employees, and senior management by visualizing yourself in the conversation.
- ➤ Verbal communication [speaking and listening] requires simple but important techniques that need to be practiced on a regular basis.
- ➤ Visualize the person or group you are talking to in the most favorable light possible.

CHAPTER FIVE

THE BOY AND THE FILBERTS

A boy put his hand into a pitcher full of filberts. He grasped as many as he could possibly hold, but when he tried to pull out his hand, he was prevented from doing so by the neck of the pitcher. Unwilling to lose his filberts, and yet unable to withdraw his hand, he burst into tears and bitterly lamented his disappointment. A bystander said to him, "Be satisfied with half the quantity, and you will readily draw out your hand."

Do not attempt too much at once

PRACTICAL APPLICATION

Even the most difficult personnel or operations problems can be successfully managed by identifying its most basic components, causes, and a well-defined and methodical process.

CASE STUDY

Jeff was happy to be promoted to a new position with more responsibility, but the new opportunity posed significant additional challenges. He quickly realized their multiple problems with employee morale, serious problems with operations efficiency, and customer complaints were on the rise. The quality of service his workgroup provided was considered to be marginal at best, and finally, operating expenses were over budget. Jeff was clearly in a challenging position, but what made matters more difficult, was his employees felt the services they were providing met standards. They were not motivated to support the efforts to improve the situation. Business for the division was declining, and senior management felt pressure to improve operations quickly.

DISCUSSION

In the case study described above, Jeff had multiple operations and personnel problems to solve. What are the first steps toward finding solutions? I have seen experienced managers try to solve all or too many circumstances at the same time. While yielding to pressure from employees or the boss to fix things, we can be tempted to make poorly targeted decisions and take action prematurely. The central message here is to recognize while in similar situations leaders need to take time to gather information, analyze the overall situation thoroughly, and establish a clearly defined game plan. Shooting at "alligators" in the pond only creates a temporary void that others will be happy to fill and exploit. Coming up with quick answers seldom results in long term solutions. Taking firm action on even a seemingly simple problem too soon can lead to an early miscue that others may be watching for – especially in Jeff's case as the new manager on the job. An insightful and accurate assessment provides for a much more reliable process.

Taking a reasonable amount of time to gain a clear sense of where to start [is] where to start. Have conversations with all the key people who can offer worthwhile information and objective insights. Management team leaders should get clarification from their managers and supervisors. Managers should have conversations with level headed employees. First, find out if all are seeing the problems in the same way. If not, find out more about the different points of view. Checking the alignment of employees' points of view about the workplace against their supervisors and managers is an essential first step. It's virtually impossible to find solutions to operations and personnel problems when everyone is seeing and interpreting the situation differently. Are there gaps in how employees' and managers' view the cause and effect of their problems? These gaps need to be discovered and resolved as soon as possible. An early objective is to get everyone or at least as many people as possible to see the circumstances [cause and symptoms] in the same way.

The point of the moment is to sort out elements Jeff believes to be the key pieces of the puzzle and be able to answer the following:

- How will he distinguish symptoms from underlying root cause?
- What are his competencies for dealing with this array of problems without additional or outside resources?
- What are the culture and core values of the workplace environment?
  o How easily will the current workplace environment welcome change that needs to occur?
- Can he take action on anything immediately to give evidence that change can happen?
- What outside resources may be available to assist if needed?
- How is progress and successes be measured?
- What are upper management's expectations regarding a timeline and benchmarks for improvements?
- Who above him in the organization is looking for improvement to occur?

As a new manager to the department, Jeff has other questions that need to be answered. One is regarding the people he will depend on to help define and implement improvements. Will they take direction? Are they committed to do what's necessary to implement change? Are they mentally strong enough to implement change? Jeff needs to know as we saw in Chapter Two to what degree, if at all, are his managers and supervisors actually a part of the problem. Answers to these questions come from open two-way conversations and applying what was outlined in Chapters One and Two. The second set of questions is about Jeff's employees. He needs to be clear about their observations so meeting and talking with them is important. But having open discussions regarding operations at meetings with employees needs to be handled with care. Jeff needs to hear how employees answer the same set of questions as he asked his managers or supervisors. Without asking directly, Jeff also needs to gain an understanding about such things as how employees view their manager and/or supervisors? To what degree are employees willing to work with managers and supervisors to implement necessary change? Are employees likely to resist efforts to make changes that are needed to improve operations? Answers to these questions will help Jeff develop an effective strategy and help him better understand the challenges and possibilities with his situation.

Now is the time for fact find and making accurate assessments summarizing the situation with Jeff's boss. Jeff needs to get his boss to make an investment in the solution with an agreement to provide a realistic timeframe for improvements to be made and provide support with resources that may be needed. Jeff's part is to give his best effort to meet expectations with positive results. This is the best time to clarify expectations and negotiate for resources that may be needed, not later.

Fishbone diagrams and various flow charts can help Jeff and his managers assess cause and effect. Sometimes this can be done with small groups of employees. Also, using what I think of as cascading questioning can be very helpful. This is simply not settling for the first answer a manager receives, especially when the answer sounds like the right answer – the one a manager is looking for. For example, a clerk may explain she takes extra time and care to – let's say double check information on incoming documents before using the data to complete her work. The employee may take pride with their diligence, but something may well be missed if a manager is happy with her short answer of, "Oh yes I always take time to double check the information I get from …. for accuracy". Hearing the employee is so compulsive or conscientious may sound great, but there is a missing piece to this conversation. It is the manager not thinking to ask the clerk how much time is spent checking for accuracy. If the manager asks this follow up question the clerk may reveal it takes her a high percentage of her time. With this second answer the manager has cause to think this situation through a little more. A third question to the clerk may be how many errors do you actually find? The answers to these cascading questions may well indicate problems with the department that is sending information. The point is taking a great sounding answer on its own value while fact finding can lead to overlooking something important. It can reveal that employees have created work-arounds to a situation that should be addressed, and that leads to inefficiencies.

Let's think about a work area that enjoys high employee morale. When asked, an employee might simply say something like things are going well, we have very few problems. But after asking one or two more questions a manager might begin to realize employees like working here because the manager allows a little too much latitude regarding employee performance. These are simple examples but they make an important point about getting all the information to assure an accurate assessment of current operating conditions. Sometimes we are simply a little too willing to be satisfied with the 1st [right] sounding answer we hear.

While asking questions, I also found it is as important to be mindful of what managers and employees *don't* say. Not hearing certain comments, descriptions, or phrases from employees and managers can be very telling. When asking employees questions about workplace environment, one typically hears descriptions and explanation that are forthcoming and positive. Employees who work in a positive environment offer favorable comments freely about operations. But, when employees and managers do not offer description of how "smoothly" their environment is functioning, I often get the sense a "a second shoe needs to be drop". Most employees are happy to say something positive about their supervisors or managers when warranted. Employees are generally eager to point out something they are happy with about their workplace, or express pride in some way during casual conversations. When responses like these are totally absent or when answers to questions seem truncated it can indicate more conversation is needed.

It's natural for Jeff to feel a little intimidated with the challenges of his new role, but his focus needs to be on getting answers to questions. His immediate responsibility is not to solve operations and personnel problems, it is to gather relevant information about the current situation and how it evolved. Armed with the information Jeff gathered through observations and two or three meetings with managers and employees. Now he or he and his managers supervisors need to sort out cause and begin to formulate an action plan. He needs to know if he can implement more than one action plan a time, and if not, he needs to know the sequence of implementing is action plans.

With his homework completed and with action plans in mind, Jeff's next step is to meet with his boss. He needs to summarize his findings and the key points that lead him to his conclusions. With support from his boss to proceed, Jeff is ready to take charge and implement his action plans.

HOW MUCH TIME SHOULD BE TAKEN TO ASSESS A SITUATION?

It may seem that the assessment regimen described above requires a lot of time, too much perhaps. It may also seem to be unnecessarily regimented. The answer may lie in the number of frustrated supervisors and managers who's attempts to resolve operations problems without such a process have only partially succeeded or failed altogether. My observations tell a high percentage of these situations involved premature decision making or were based on the wrong assumptions. In this instance, after making a thorough assessment, Jeff was able to gather the information he needed, identify the key issues, and wisely assessed the situation. These steps helped him visualize specific action plans in less than a months' time. Considering the long-standing issues, the department was experiencing a month's [delay] seems to fit into a very reasonable timeline. The reconnaissance time for Jeff was actually short considering number of department issues he had to resolve. This means all preconceived notions about cause and effect should be wiped clean or validated through a fact-finding process.

Talking point when meeting with employees, managers, and supervisors to assess alignment of the issues:

- What is working well and what is not?
    - Get examples.
    - What are the contributing factors

- Get points of view regarding underlying causes
    - Ask follow up questions

- Assess employee morale
    - Get examples that help characterize employee morale
    - Ask questions that can clarify employee morale level.
- Ask employees what improvements could improve their work environment.
- Are there individual employee standouts, both positive and negative?
    - Employees who are looking for change may be encouraged to help facilitate change in some way.
    - It might be helpful to have a discussion with the employees who are not encouraged to see change in order to understand why
- Understand the manager's and supervisor's competencies.
    - Be sure to have their support

MANAGING ANTAGONISTS

Keeping a group of employees focused while trying to get answers to operations and personnel questions, especially during group meetings can be difficult. Facilitators, whether they are managers or trained facilitators cannot allow comments that degrade the quality of discussion. Antagonists who make aggressive or passive aggressive comments and accusations create a sour environment that disrupts the flow of worthwhile information gathering. Facilitators need to watch for this negative conduct and address it directly and promptly. Such attempts can be shut down by restating the purpose of the discussion. The need is for objective and clearly focused observations and experiences rather than focusing on people who may have been involved. It is also very helpful to, as much as possible, encourage comments to be stated in the context of no fault. Why, because people generally do things for a reason. It is more productive to question the reason for the individual's action rather than the person. The focus needs to be solely on issues, not individuals. If the person is problem employee in general, the facilitator will be able to make that determination later and the individual's performance issues can be addressed at a more appropriate time.

Solutions Can't Stand on Their Own

Finally, Jeff needs to be sure his action plans have the proper underpinning. For example, developing an excellent new set of procedures to improve the efficiency of a service or quality of a product would be useless if the need for developing employee competencies to function in that environment were not considered. Another example may be when implementing an initiative to improve employee morale with posters, an employee recognition plan, and better work scheduling, etc. Without making sure managers have a supportive mind set to manage the new environment, the effort will be short lived or at least minimized. Great ideas need to be accompanied with the proper under pinning and support system. These examples may seem obvious and very basic, yet it's surprising how often nicely developed action plans and initiatives have fallen short because the underpinning was not considered seriously enough.

CHAPTER SUMMARY

- ➤ When confronted with several problems, resist the temptation to tackle all or many at the same time.
  - o Take time to make objective assessments with the help of other key department employees if possible.
  - o Determine which of the problems [if any] can be packaged and addressed at the same time or need to be addressed separately.

- ➤ Get everyone on the same page with cause and effect of the problems
  - o Employees' points of view regarding problems need to be aligned with those of the managers and supervisors.

- ➤ Meet with managers and employees to get their description of the problems.
  - o List the key issues <u>on a wall board</u> if possible and clarify their contributing elements.
  - o Be clear about the order or sequence for implementing action plans.

- ➤ Be clear about the resources that may be needed.
  - o Make provisions to strengthen the competencies of managers, supervisor, and employees if higher performance standards are expected.

- ➤ Research best practices and consider how they can be incorporated into the action plan.
- ➤ Clearly visualize how each element of the plan is expected to function when fully implemented.
- ➤ Set achievable timelines for solving the various problems.
- ➤ Make accurate assessments of current circumstances using the fact-finding regimen outlined in this chapter.
- ➤ Keep the boss informed

- o Be clear about the procedure for making a thorough assessment of the problems
- o Be clear about timelines and expectations
- o Request resources that may be needed.

- ➢ Create an environment of open and two-way communication with employees and management personnel.
- ➢ Review the final action plan in detail with managers, employees, and the boss.
- ➢ Be willing to take advice and make adjustments to the action plan where indicated.
- ➢ Be clear about indicators that can be used to verify progress.
- ➢ Be mindful of and manage antagonists directly.
- ➢ Mastery of the details leads to better decisions. It doesn't require a lot of additional time and does not need to delay decision making.

CHAPTER SIX

THE MOUNTAINS IN LABOUR

One day the Countrymen noticed that the Mountains were in labour; smoke came out of their summits, the earth was quaking at their feet, trees were crashing, and huge rocks were tumbling. They felt sure that something horrible was going to happen. They all gathered together in one place to see what terrible thing this could be. They waited and they waited, but nothing came. At last there was a still more violent earthquake, and a huge gap appeared in the side of the Mountains. They all fell down upon their knees and waited. At last, and at last, a teeny, tiny mouse poked its little head and bristles out of the gap and came running down towards them, and ever after they used to say:

Much outcry, little outcome.

Practical Application

Leaders should not allow employees and sometimes managers to develop creative work-arounds in order to avoid and delay the implementation of permanent solutions to on-going dysfunctional operational or personnel problems.

Case Study

Sam is the manager of a service that performs complex medical interventional procedures. The complexity and time needed to complete these procedures ranges from thirty-minutes to greater than four hours. The physicians who perform these services are recognized by the hospital's medical staff as being very talented and skilled. They also enjoy national recognition for using cutting-edge techniques when performing these procedures. They have published articles in major medical journals, presented lectures, and teach residence.

A talented support staff of technologists and nurses work with the physicians to provide vascular interventional (repair) throughout the body including the brain. The technologists report to a technical manager and the nursing staff reports to a licensed and experienced acute-care nurse manager.

Despite the competencies of these three distinct work groups and the recognition they enjoy, there are long-standing and simmering workplace issues with inefficiencies that too often cause major delays between procedures, low morale, and cost containment problems. Physicians view the patient-care competencies of the nurses and technical staff as being very satisfactory, but they point to their poor management skills as the reason for the inefficient operation and the general dysfunction of the service. However, both the nurses and technologists view the physicians as being the principle cause of the confused and dysfunctional workplace because the physicians do not follow operational guidelines and rules. Morale among technologists and nurses is low.

The managers conducted multiple meetings with their staff in an attempt to sort out and resolve and to improve their operations issues and improve cooperation among all three groups. The lead physician would occasionally attend these meetings, but no matter how well the discussions seemed to progress, operations continued with virtually no improvement as frustrations of all continued for more than a year. Below is a summary of their complaints they could agree on.

- The MDs are not available when the patient is ready to start a procedure.
- Leadership of the lead MD is not consistent.
- The MDs felt the nurses and technologists are not working together so the patients are not always ready when the MDs arrives to begin procedures.
- Supplies and instruments, such as sterile trays, are sometimes not ready or immediately available when needed during a procedure.
- Patient schedules are seldom followed because of add-on cases
- The MDs book cases without first consulting or giving notice to the floor coordinator
- The technologists have concerns about the leadership of their manager.

Despite these simmering internal problems, outside observers including referring physicians and patients viewed the quality of the medical work accomplished as exceptional. Sometimes extraordinary efforts are needed by all three groups to create space in an already full schedule to accommodate an emergent procedure. In fact, it is the type of service where emergency add-on cases are common. Ironically it is during these adverse pressured times when everyone pulls together instinctively and procedures are completed very efficiently. These efforts contribute strongly to the professional pride everyone has with what they do, and the quality of lifesaving services they perform routinely as a group. Despite the operations problems and frustrations, employee turnover is surprising low. Their pride and dedication encourage them to compensate and "stay with it".

DISCUSSION

What we see in this scenario are three defined groups who are competing for control and using various finger-pointing techniques to explain the dysfunction of operations. Their explanations for the cause of problems are intended to off load responsibility and distance themselves from accountability. Too often their problem-solving meetings were filled with anecdotes that accomplished little but shunt accountability. They respected each other's individual medical competencies but saw their operations management issues as something very different. The nurses and technologists learned to build in creative work-arounds to compensate for the unresolved core issues. But by doing so they unwittingly laid traps for themselves by relying on the work-arounds to get everyone through the day. It also seemed to provide a kind of rationale for delaying hard action that could fix their core problems.

The smoldering mountain in the fable symbolizes what these frustrations may lead to, a catastrophic incident, which eventually and finally brings everyone to the table with a new reality that their operations problems must be solved. We have seen these simmering mountain scenarios occur in all industries, from airlines, automobile, medicine, and oil to name just a few. The willingness to resolve issues did not occur until the reality of a catastrophic event became too costly to continue as they were. Fortunately, with the case study that event had been avoided.

GETTING EVERYONE TOGETHER

The medical director of the service did not have total authority for managing the physicians in his group. Also, his rotating schedule made it difficult to attend all the problem-solving meetings which complicated the situation further. E-mail communications were used to keep everyone posted about meeting content but this was not a good substitute for key people not attending. After several of failed meetings a strongly worded email was sent by the division director that summarized the situation and brought everyone to the table to find real solutions. It addressed the lack of commitments all were willing to make, and it called for the two managers and physician leader to accept responsibility for their part of the problem and commit to defining new operating procedures and commitments. The email called for an end to use of anecdotes and accusations to shut responsibility, and reminded managers that having meetings is not taking action. Despite the approximately 5 meetings that were actually held no such commitments had been discussed.

Establishing standards and commitments is essential to solving any operational problem and the simmering problems in this case study makes that very clear. Sometimes the competency of those who need to follow new standards and operational commitments may be in question. Fortunately, that was not the situation with this case study. But it is something to take into account when new action plans are being considered. There was one other complication that sometimes occurs when workgroup leaders need to define new operating procedures and standards. Managers are sometimes reluctant to yield to what best practice in order to "hold the line" for their employee's. Managers are sometimes reluctant to appear to their employees as "giving in" and do what may be indicated and necessary. It is at this point when the group's facilitator needs to work with managers in order to get maximum cooperation. There is no question an element of this complicated the need to establish new operation expectations. Sometimes, it is a difficult position for a manager to be in, but the decision must be driven by making an objective value judgement regarding the overall benefit[s] of a proposed change versus a given department's interests.

CHAPTER SUMMARY

➤ Identify each of the operations and personnel problems, list them, and get validation from those involved.

➤ Use various tools such as fishbone analysis, root cause analysis, flow charts etc. to objectively separate symptoms from root cause.

➤ Be clear about how each problem impacts operating costs such as overtime, wasted supplies, staff morale, staff turnover, quality of service or product, and morale.

➤ Meet with key personnel separately to talk through issues they are most concerned with

➤ Be clear about system support processes.
  o Adjustments to patient scheduling procedures
  o Review various supply processes such as ordering supplies, inventory control, paper flow available equipment needs to perform procedures.
  o Provide additional training if indicated

➤ Develop a draft plan and review with key personnel along with a reality check regarding what is actually achievable.
  o Be willing to take advice and make adjustments where indicated.

➤ Develop monitoring tools to measure success

➤ Scheduling meeting[s] should not be thought of as – taking action. Long standing operations and personnel problems are not resolved by having multiple meetings where anecdotes are repeated with little forward thinking about defining specific objectives, standards of performance, and commitments to meet those standards.

➤ Set specific performance standards and expectations, and institute clearly defined action for noncompliance.

➤ Research Best Practice and build as many best practice elements into the final operations plan as possible.

CHAPTER SEVEN

THE YOUNG THIEF
AND HIS MOTHER

*A young Man had been caught in a daring act of theft and
had been condemned to be executed for it. He expressed his
desire to see his Mother, and to speak with her before he was
led to execution, and of course this was granted. When his
Mother came to him he said: "I want to whisper to you," and
when she brought her ear near him, he nearly bit it off. All
the bystanders were horrified, and asked him what he could*

79

mean by such brutal and inhuman conduct. "It is to punish her," he said. "When I was young I began with stealing little things, and brought them home to Mother. Instead of rebuking and punishing me, she laughed and said: "It will not be noticed." It is because of her that I am here to-day." "He is right, woman," said the Priest; "the Lord hath said:

'Train up a child in the way he should go; and when he is old he will not depart therefrom.'"

PRACTICAL APPLICATION

A central responsibility of a leader is to train, mentor, and coach. They are also accountable for employees' performance.

CASE STUDY

Sally, a department manager of an important and large department within her company had been getting upsetting feedback about the quality of services they provide. She also became aware of complaints from employees within the group. Some felt they were doing more in order to compensate for the errors of their coworkers, while others blamed their supervisors for not pitching in to help do the work. Those who were viewed as doing less and causing the majority of errors felt put upon by the complaints they received from the supervisors. The situation reached a point where the number of errors in combination with poor employee morale had to be addressed directly and effectively.

The work group is required to provide a wide range of highly medical imaging services where each procedure required a unique skill set. Each employee received their initial training from certified schools. Despite this, employees were making errors with increasing frequency. Their supervisors were becoming more and more frustrated that their pleas and attempts at discipline yielded very little improvement. It became even more confusing and frustrating for supervisors when they approached some of their employees about specific errors and found the employee clearly had the knowledge and skill set to perform the task without errors.

DISCUSSION

Employees used high tech imaging equipment that are entirely computer-driven to perform an array of medical tests. To operate the machine employees, have to make various setting changes on the control panel during each procedure. The procedures performed in the department range from approximately 20 minutes to 2 hours. During each procedure employees often referred to procedure books to be sure machine the machine setting they made aware correct.

The department was experiencing a growing number of errors that affected quality of test results. Also, something was happening that seemed to defy explanation. Not only was the frequency of errors increasing, the errors were made by employees who were known to be well trained and conscientious. Knowing this, Sally assumed her employees were being careless and she began to implement progressive discipline. A few weeks of using this approach had no impact on the frequency or type of errors, and in addition, her employees were angry saying her discipline was arbitrary and miss guided.

The atmosphere became contentious and Sally called for assistance from the organization's HR department. A trained facilitator, Jonathan was assigned to work with Sally to help get to the bottom of the problem and find solutions. Sally gave Jonathan an initial briefing and he proceeded to schedule a series of meetings with Sally's employees. The value of having an "outside" person facilitating the meeting allowed for a less contentious discussion and a more objective scenario for fact finding. The employees agreed the number of errors was increasing and emphasized they were also upset by what was happening. Sally only listened and held her comments. She knew there would be time later for clarification.

Jonathan's meeting with the employees identified the following:

- Employees were expected to know how to make settings on the control panel for more than fifty different tests.
- The tests performed ranged widely in complexity and time needed to complete.
- The range of complexity required employees to have a broad set of skills.
- Each test had its own set of rules about how the control panel needed to be set.

Sally and Jonathan felt they understand better what their employees were seeing and feeling. They knew all of their complaints may not be entirely valid, but for the moment that was not relevant, it was to get and understand the employees' views about what was happening and their thoughts on why. After getting feedback from her employees, it became clear to Sally that employee experience and certification of competencies does not assure high quality work. She began to consider a lack of training and other on-the-job factors her employees talked about may be contributing to the errors. She also realized that despite her employees' formal training and certified skill sets, a more thorough evaluation of their competency is needed with respect to the tests they had to perform. They also had to consider the work environment issues as being a contributing factor. Sally and her supervisors began by making a careful assessment of employee skill sets.

Sally reviewed with her supervisors all the procedures the department performed and soon realized the complexity of those procedures corresponded to very different employee skill sets and training needs. In fact, five specific skill levels were defined and five very different training programs had to established. Employee training had been packed into a general course for new employees with the assumption that the new employee's certification was sufficient validation for them to perform all the department's procedures. Sally thought any remaining training for specific procedures would occur via the buddy system. She didn't realize her own employees were not fully capable to be trainers.

Then Sally and her supervisors reviewed the errors from the past six months with each employee who caused them. These were one-on-one interviews with the employees and their supervisor to see if more specific cause and effect could be discovered. These conversations would also help Sally and her supervisors design new training courses. The interviews were conducted in a relaxed and non-intimidating manner with clear emphasis on the need to gain an understanding about the contributing factors rather than point blame. This fact-finding process was acknowledged by the employees and was completed in two weeks' time. An analysis of errors along with the employees' input made clear that discipline was not the answer.

Sally and Johnathan's fact finding began to shed light on one of the ironies which was why a few of Sally's most competent employees were making errors. It was something that had been mentioned indirectly by employees. There were two control panels in a relatively small work area so as many as six coworkers could be talking and working next to the person operating the control panel. The work area also served as the department's central observation and gathering area. So, employees could be distracted while working at the control panels. Unfortunately, because of the work area's dual function in the department there was no other space available. With this Sally began to understand how easy it was for some employees to be distracted by peripheral activity and conversations and simply lose focus during the procedure which caused them to omit making machine settings. The missing piece to understanding this irony was a few of her well-trained employees could not stay focused because of the distractions in the area. Sally realized no amount of training or disciplinary action could compensate.

CONCLUSION AND FOLLOW UP NOTES

With the information gathered, Jonathan and Sally began to visualize the action plan that was needed. First, a new training regimen needed to emphasize competencies for all five levels of procedures their department performed, which included a few high-level procedures that were recently added to the department's service. Second, the procedures books which had many hand-written almost scribbled notes needed to be updated and re-written. Also, additional copies needed to be placed in convenient locations around each of the control panels to allow quick access. Revisions needed to be made on an on-going basis by supervisors. The fourth element was more difficult because Sally had to address the situation with her employees who were not able to work in a hectic environment. It was clear no amount of training could correct the problem. These employees were offered two possible options. On was reassigned to another location where similar procedures were performed but where the pace is slower and work environment is much calmer. Sally could not allow continued errors, so the second option for the employee[s] was to leave employment and Sally would allow reasonable time for that to happen. Of the three employees who were given these options, two found similar work with another organization and one was reassigned to the other inhouse location. Other helpful conditions were established for Sally's employees.

- Employees who needed additional training were permitted to select employees who were approved by their supervisor to train.
- Two months of additional paid time was granted for employees to work with their designated trainer to upgrade their skills
- Each employee who required training was given two months' time to upgrade their skills and get validation to perform all five categories of procedures.
- Skill sets for all employees had to be validated by Sally's supervisors.

The following months saw a notable decrease in errors. There was a sense among employees the work distribution problem they described to Johnathan had been virtually resolved. The stress that had developed among employees and their supervisors lessened considerably.

As with the fable and case study, strong discipline [putting employee's in jail] is not a good substitute for fixing quality of performance issues. Very often there are extenuating circumstances that need to be addressed which contribute to the problem. Managers should not assume employee certifications fully validate employee competencies and capabilities. Conversations at staff meeting should occasionally include a brief conversation about issues that relate to the need for training. This case study shows how Sally's willingness to pause, listen carefully to her employees, and take time to fact find and objectively assess cause and effect made all the difference in the outcome. It helped to create an environment where employees felt more comfortable on the job and where discussing skill sets and competencies was not considered to be a threat.

CHAPTER SUMMARY

➢ Be mindful that taking disciplinary action may not necessarily be the first step to correct employee performance issues.

➢ Make an objective and reasonably detailed assessment of working conditions, access to equipment, and general environment.

 o Make reasonable changes to create the best possible working conditions.

➢ Know the details of the task's employees perform.

 o Be sure employees' formal training is sufficient to support current performance standards.

 o Provide reasonable conditions and opportunities for employee training that may be needed.

 o Consider providing additional paid time for employee training if needed

 o Set realistic timelines for employees to achieve the required competencies

 o Allow employee's with validated competencies to train coworkers

 o Allow for proper buddy system training conditions

CHAPTER EIGHT

BELLING THE CAT

Long ago, the mice had a general council to consider what measures they could take to outwit their common enemy, the Cat. Some said this, and some said that; but at last a young mouse got up and said he had a proposal to make, which he thought would meet the case. "You will all agree," said he, "that our chief danger consists in the sly and treacherous manner in which the enemy approaches us. Now, if we could receive some signal of her approach, we could easily escape from her. I venture, therefore, to propose that a small bell be procured, and attached by a ribbon round the neck of the Cat.

By this means we should always know when she was about, and could easily retire while she was in the neighborhood."

This proposal met with general applause, until an old mouse got up and said:

"That is all very well, but who is to bell the Cat?" The mice looked at one another and nobody spoke. Then the old mouse said:

"It is easy to propose impossible remedies."

PRACTICAL APPLICATION

When considering new plans of action, no matter how complex or simple, people are as important as the process.

CASE STUDY

Howard had been working as the director of a major service within a hospital, and was asked to take over the in-patient transportation service in addition to his current responsibilities. The service conducted a high volume of patient transports throughout the hospital and was experiencing growing complaints about the unpredictability of patient pickup and deliveries to and from nursing floors and various diagnostic areas. Howard's principle objective was to establish a scheduling procedure that would lead to a more reliable service.

A workgroup of department heads and nurses who were experiencing problems met to assess the situation and develop an action plan. After the second meeting members of the workgroup felt they had a good handle on the problem and it would be relatively easy to solve. The transporters were experienced, hard working, and eager to work with a new operations plan. A new computer driven scheduling application was purchased and installed. A new digital communication system was also purchased, installed and ready to use. It was expected to provide quick communication between transport dispatcher and tracked transporters while on route with patients. Having this information allowed the dispatcher to better schedule new assignments and keep the departments better informed of patient pick-up and delivery times. The transporter's procedure manual was also updated.

An announcement was sent with confidence to all nursing floors and directors of diagnostic services that a new scheduling and communications system was developed and will be implemented very soon. The first day of operations with the new system indicated some hope for its success, but by the third day, it was not showing the expected results. In fact, the new operations plan with its new communications system created several additional problems and solved none of the old problems. The implementation proved to be a disaster, and the value of money spent for the new tracking application and communication system was very quickly questioned by senior management.

DISCUSSION

As we see with the fable *Belling the Cat*, great ideas alone were not enough to solve the mouse's problems. Even great sounding ideas have to be tested with people who have hands on experience. The people who actually performed patient transport services in the hospital had not been consulted or invited to participate in the planning meetings. The ideas for solutions and plan that evolved was based solely on manager's observations and experiences. The solutions were targeted perfectly to those assumptions but the outcome was embarrassing. The problem was the managers didn't know – what they didn't know and let their confidence and enthusiasm lead them. They didn't take in account underlying issues transporters had to deal with throughout the day. Howard felt perfectly comfortable and confident about how the great sounding ideas he heard for solutions hit all the buttons.

After the unsuccessful implementation follow up meetings were scheduled with three transporters attending. The transporters discussed the various details of their job and helped the workgroup find ways to address the troublesome scenario. After the second meeting with the transporters the following new issues were fully recognized.

- Transporters spent approximately 50 percent of their time not transporting because they are looking for wheelchairs and litters.
- An estimated 15 percent of wheelchairs and litters were not usable because they were dirty, broken, or poorly equipped with needed accessories.
- The newly developed transporters' schedule did not give the nurses on patient floors or employees in the various diagnostic department adequate notice of a pending patient arrival. This meant transporters spent a lot of time waiting for patients to be changed and ready for the procedure.
- Patient transport delays sometimes caused studies to be rescheduled for another day which increased patients' length of stay.
- Nurses were sometimes not able to administrator exam preps in sufficient time which also caused tests to be rescheduled.
- Despite their time on the job, transporters needed additional training in;
  o Handling emergent-patient situations while on route
  o Basic language training so they could communicate and better understand patients.
  o Transporters also needed additional in-service training on body mechanics to help reduce the physical strain while lifting and moving patients.

With all the relevant information now on the table, the managers and transporters were able to define all the important elements of their job that needed to be addressed.

- A designated area in the facility where all wheelchairs and litters would be stored when not in use.
- A technician was needed to repair broken wheelchairs and litters.
- The new digital communication and transporter tracking system needed to be tweaked.

- The physical therapy department was asked to assess and define a body mechanics training program to help transporters move patients and prevent injury.
- A more detailed description of the program and the implementation plan was written and sent to all clinical areas of the hospital.
- A few monitoring tools were defined to help measure the success of the program after implementation.

Having all the stake holders accounted for is the only way to assure the best possible outcome. Enthusiasm that sometimes comes with taking on a new initiative can narrow the scope of fact finding and assessment processes. "Why waste time getting someone else involved who is on the periphery or just a line worker?" "They will only raise issues unnecessarily and complicate the process." There have been occasions when the facilitator avoided inviting people because he / she didn't want someone else "tampering" with what surely seemed to be a brilliant plan.

CHAPTER SUMMARY

- ➤ Make a list of key personnel in the organization who may be affected by the final plan and invite them to participate in an initial assessment group meeting.
- ➤ Document the key elements [especially the key three or four issues] of the problem that need to be improved or solved and don't lose sight of them throughout the process.
    - o Be sure these elements are adequately addressed in the action plan

- ➤ Invite those who will be primarily impacted by the plan to review and critique the action plan early enough to allow for adjustments.
    - o Perform an honest reality check against the comments and advice of stake holders
    - o Define how the outcome will be evaluated and validated.
    - o Measure outcome directly against those top the key elements that need to be improved.

- ➤ Make sure all those who will responsible for implementing the plan are adequately trained and capable.
- ➤ Consider and secure the underpinning items that are needed to support and maintain the plan after implementation.
- ➤ Track progress with clearly defined way points that need to be reached.
    - o Celebrate milestones reached during planning and implementation.

CHAPTER NINE

THE FOX AND GOAT

Once a fox was roaming in the dark. As ill luck would have it, he fell into a well. He tried his best to come out but all to no use. So, he had to remain there till the next morning.

At about fore-noon the next day, a goat came that way. She peeped into the well and saw the fox there.

"What are you doing there, Mr. Fox?" asked the goat.

"I came here to drink water. It is the best I have ever tasted. Come and see for yourself," replied the sly fox.

Without thinking even a bit, the goat jumped into the
well. She quenched her thirst and looked for a way to get out.
The fox said, "I've an idea. Stand on your hind legs.
I'll climb on your head and get out. Then I shall help you
out too." The silly goat did so and the fox got out of the well.
While walking away, he said," Had you been wise, you
would never have got in without seeing how to get out."

Look before you leap

PRACTICAL APPLICATION

People often fear change, but many times it's not the change itself they fear or resist.

CASE STUDY

This case study is about a large organization that had several departments where very specialized products were made. Each department functioned under a management model that allowed a high degree of autonomy to its department managers. A Key responsibility of each manager was to handle customer service problems. Management reports indicated the company enjoyed a good customer satisfaction record overall. Despite this, the company's reputation for making quality products ranked in the mid range among its competitors.

Although the company has been reasonably efficient overall, and customer service has been acceptable, senior management felt there was room for improvement and saw the need to make changes. Senior management decided to move all customer satisfaction services to a central Quality Service Department. Here customer complaints could be handled more efficiently and with lower operating expenses. The vision was this restructuring would also provide better customer satisfaction services and over time improve the quality of their products through more focused feedback to product designers. Although senior

94

management felt the scope of these changes was moderate the proposed changes were not viewed by department managers in the same way.

A senior manager was appointed to be the principal architect of these changes and was designated to be the lead person and principal change agent for the initiative. Resistance from department managers began to grow almost immediately. Cries of "breaking a system that is working" were loud and clear. Questions were raised about how such a diverse product line of products with their unique characteristics could be centralized. How could the employees in the new department possibly handle the array of questions and understand the unique characteristics of each product? How could a centralized group of employees be so knowledgeable to address all customer complaints and questions? Other concerns about breaking down the current level of department efficiencies were raised. What was not voiced and was an issue that was important to each department manager. Their perceived diminished scope of authority. Although managers did not point to this openly, it was an important issue for them.

DISCUSSION

We often hear that people resist and at times deliberately work to avoid change. Comments such as, "People don't change" or "You can't change a tiger's stripes" are common. Why is this apparent avoidance to change so common, especially in a business setting? The reason may not be the proposed change itself. People make changes all the time. We change where we live. We change the type of music we like and the people we dislike and then come to like. Even when unfortunate events change our lives, we usually have some choices available which allows us to feel at least a minimal sense of control over the situation. But, when we anticipate change at work, that sense of control is absent.

One of the strongest human impulses that is embedded in our human nature is an aversion to be harmed or diminished in some way. Our human nature drives us to maintain control and avoid losses. In a workplace environment, individuals frequently sense a loss of control with proposed changes. Chapter Two covers different and important expectations managers have compared to employees so when managers move to impose change, internal alarms almost automatically go off with employees. Employees know they have virtually no options or choices they can exercise with pending change and this creates a sense of uncertainty and insecurity. It works against the basic survival instincts.

Fortunately, most often the impact we feel is minimal but even the mere suggestion of change tweaks our human nature. It reminds us of our survival instincts and depending on the circumstances, we sometimes look for ways to resist. The point here is managers often confuse what looks like resistance to [change] with these human instincts to survive and stay whole. The result can be frustration all around until those concerns are addressed in a reasonable fashion. However, plans for an organization to make changes can become more complicated than necessary if managers assume the resistance, they sense is purely about the change itself.

For example, the change may evoke a fear of an individual or group of individuals losing influence in the workplace. Another proposed change may create an unfamiliar work environment that challenges an employee's competency because of higher performance expectations. Other types of proposed organization and operations changes may signal an employee's sense of position in the organization. An individual or group of employees may feel their pride [identity] in their organization may be diminished. None of these concerns [are about] the change – they are about the human instincts. My response on occasion to employee concerns is to ask them if they were hired after the proposed change was implemented, how would they feel about the new process or procedure? In virtually all cases, the employees would answer.... I would probably be OK with it.

In many instances, rather than managers arguing to justify the benefits of a proposed change, their time would be better spent talking with employees and addressing their legitimate concerns. Most often employees can see the benefits of a proposed change. They understand businesses have a responsibility to generate sufficient income to cover expenses and grow in order to grow and keep pace with their competitors. To meet these challenges objectives and processes are always subject to change. Mission statements need to be revised, and new company objectives may be needed. These are an organization's survival tools. The central point here is when leaders take time to address the realities of employees' concerns regarding the change, implementation can often occur with less complications and less lost time. This does not, by any means, suggest organizations should avoid change because of employees' concerns, it means employees' concerns need to be recognized and managed and accounted for in a reasonable manner. By doing so employees are likely to be more willing to support what has been proposed.

On the surface one may ask why is this concern really necessary. You may ask why is it important or even a relevant? "Change needs to happen, just let it happen." Is a common theme. The answer lays with many managers who experienced unnecessary delays, derailed and unfortunate outcomes, or totally failed attempts because their employees never really got on board. The reason for these problems was because the change agents didn't understand something very basic which is; **people are as important as the process.** In this case study, the primary focus was given to all the details of the proposed change which often included a tight implementation schedule, but not the employees' reasonable concerns. As a result, the initiative had a hard time getting off the planning table.

Eleanor Roosevelt is credited for saying "Happiness is not the goal; it is a by-product". If we apply this bit of wisdom when planning for organizational and operations changes, we can broaden its meaning by saying the *goal is not success*, the goal is to plan wisely to account for *all* the pieces of the puzzle. By doing so success will be the more likely outcome. If problems do occur along the way, they are more likely to be managed with less complications. People are a very important part of the process. Timelines are almost always an important element of a proposed change. Fortunately, in almost all situations, accounting for all the pieces of the puzzle can be satisfied without threatening the timeline of the proposed change.

Creating A Positive Environment
for Change

The workplace environment needs to be suitable – able to support the change in order to have a relatively easy and successful outcome. Here are a few key elements that if taken into account can prepare a workplace for the stresses that can dome with change.

- Does the organization's culture support change?
  o Do employees generally understand the pressures and challenges from outside competition that puts current operations at a disadvantage without the proposed change?
  o Have employee training completed before implementation so they can meet the new challenges and performance standards?
- Does the organization have financial, personnel, and equipment resources for making changes that are needed?
- Does the organization's management personnel have the skill set to;
  o Assess the need for the right change to occur
  o Do managers have the required skill set to plan and implement change.
- Does upper management recognize and support an operating philosophy that people [employees] are as important as the process?

People Are as Important as the Process

The time needed to give appropriate attention to people and address their basic expectations and concerns requires less time than one would imagine. This should not be thought of as an [additional] or separate effort from the core initiative. Here are two examples. A reasonable employee expectation is to get updated information about things like how plans are progressing, possible timelines, who to contact with questions, etc. It would be difficult to provide ongoing two-way conversation with all who may have these questions and concerns.

But building answers to these and other issues about a project can be accomplished with relative ease by sending a [project update letter] via email or even a chat site that could be built inhouse. Doing so allows employees to get answers to questions without interrupting progress. Overall it can provide an appropriate opportunity for employees to feel a part of the project and understand the care that is taken during assessment, planning, and implementation phases. All of which helps to build a measure of confidence in everyone involved that can increase the likeliness for their cooperation and support. The needed time and effort to accomplish this is minimal and the benefits this provides out weight the risks one may anticipate.

Another way to address employee concerns is to create opportunities for open two-way conversations. Here project facilitators can address valid employee concerns and have open dialogue about how the change may impact them and what can be to minimize the impact. These could be important events that help employees learn how they can best cope with employee concerns. These discussions can add a human element to the process that employees will appreciate.

TWO WAY COMMUNICATION

As noted above, establishing good two-way communication is essential to a successful plan for operations changes. I have seen leaders let their elevated enthusiasm for getting a project up and running avoid taking [extra time] to allow for open two-way communication with those who may be affected. This can obviously lead to embarrassing trips back to the drawing board and lost time. These mishaps also break down confidence in the project leaders that can lead to employees being less willing to do their very best during the changeover. As the fable in this chapter suggests, leaders can avoid a multitude of unnecessary problems and embarrassments by looking thoroughly before leaping. The simple act of dismissing what may seem to be a less important piece and assuming all the pieces to the puzzle have been accounted for - in the name of moving quickly - can have a disproportionately negative impact on the outcome.

Here are a few key points that can help planners avoid common traps that can lead to a less successful outcome.

Eight Basic Steps for Achieving Successful Outcome for Change

- Establish convenient opportunity for on-going two-way communication.
  - o Be clear about why a change is important
    - Use objective measurements to assess the benefits of a proposed change
    - Show how continuing without change can impact the organization and its employees
  - o Explain with as much clarity as possible the reality of losses and gains employees will experience after implementation.
    - Address how expected losses can be minimized and managed in the best way possible with the new operating scenario.
    - Define how the success of the outcome will be measured.

- Summarize which resources will be needed and are available.
  - o Outline the financial, personnel, and equipment resources that are available.
  - o Discuss how other departments will be affected.
  - o Consider having the leader help with planning and implementation

- Provide a clear timeline for key milestones to be reached during planning and implementation
  - o Discuss in reasonable detail how each of these key project phases will be met
  - o Discuss backup plans

- Talk about the project leaders
  - o Identify project leaders who are involved with planning and who will be on-site overseeing implementation.

- Be clear about the organization's commitment to implement change
- Have a clear understanding of industry best practice and include as many of those elements during planning

SELECTING PROJECT MANAGERS

Choosing the [right] project managers[s] is obviously an important piece of the puzzle. Unfortunately, sometimes the criteria for the best choices are based on personal relationships or an individual's political standing in the organization rather than specific leadership competencies. What criteria should be used to make the best selections? The first would be select people who have established a strong management profile. A review of the information in Chapters One and Two would be helpful.

Senior managers should be clear about which leadership personality traits would be best suited for a given project. Complex broad scope operations changes require a project manager who can keep overall progress of critical pieces in clear focus. Be able to see the forest for the trees, and who knows how to delegate. Someone who can accurately gauge progress without getting in the way while maintaining overall control is an important skill. With projects that require leaders who will work directly with employees on the front lines, project managers must be able to exercise a different set of skills. They must be detail oriented and able to analyze and accurately assess progress of individual pieces of the puzzle. And, they must be able to exchange information and details of the initiative accurately, effectively, and directly. They must have good communication skills with employees – and in a manner that encourages their support and cooperation. It is especially important that selected managers have the trust of upper management throughout.

EVALUATING OUTCOME

Virtually all initiatives are intended to achieve something worthwhile if not something that is essential to the organizations. So, it is important to track on-going progress during planning and implementation by using simple tools that can accurately gauge progress and success. Benchmarks with their timelines should be defined during the earliest stages of planning and built into the monitoring tools. It is the scope and complexity of a given initiative that determines the number and the level of details needed for benchmarking progress and success of outcome. I found it helpful to have a designated individual track and provide alerts when these benchmarks are satisfied or missed. The person chosen to monitor these needs full access to the flow of communication and be able to draw attention at the earliest possible time to key people who are overseeing the project.

Planners can choose from an array of techniques and dashboard designs that are available. Benchmarks are not to be established casually. To be most useful they need to have; 1, A well-defined expectation that is achievable; 2, A realistic timeline; 3, Easy to use monitoring tools; 4, A defined procedure to alert the senior project manager. The more detailed benchmarks are set, the more rigidly they need to be tracked and accounted for.

Managing Feedback During Planning and Implementation

On-site managers must have the capacity to objectively evaluate feedback from all those who are involved, including employees. As "Canaries in the mine" first line employees are in a key position to make worthwhile observations that should not be overlooked. Making accurate assessments of small or seemingly inconsequential situations may later turn out to be important missions. The temptation to avoid feedback from unlikely places can also prove to be an embarrassing omission. Unfortunately, there are no hard rules for sorting worthwhile versus nonsense from antagonists. Leaders need to use commonsense, a measure of wisdom gained from past experiences to gauge the "look" and "feel" of feedback.

Initial Talking Points with Employees Regarding A Proposed Change in Operations

❖ Understand and provide an honest, fact-based accounting of current circumstances.
  ➢ Why does the current process / procedure not support the organization's mission, vision, or operating objectives?

❖ With as much clarity and openness as possible, discuss the estimated actual losses individuals or workgroups are likely to experience. If possible, describe how these losses can be managed or minimized
  ➢ Be forthright about key project issues which may cause a degree of discomfort to "air". Be open to discuss these issues. The conversations may be uncomfortable, but necessary.

❖ Discuss timelines.
❖ Outline training issues that may be needed for all those involved and other resources such as equipment.
❖ Introduce the project leaders

8 IMPORTANT CONSIDERATIONS WHEN PLANNING FOR CHANGE

The enthusiasm for success that sometimes comes when planning a change in operations or embarking on a new of initiative can carry the risk of overlooking or taking seemingly insignificant issues for granted. Here are nine points change agents may want to consider and address before a plan is finalized.

❖ Make a thorough assessment of the need for change
  o Be able to define the specific elements of current operations that point to the need for change against what is expected when the change is fully implemented.
  o Evaluate the organization's or department's readiness for change
    ▪ Does the culture fit and support the new conditions?

- Is the vision for change shared by the key people in the organization?
- Are sufficient human, financial, and equipment resources available?

❖ Be clear about the core benefits of the proposed change or new initiative.
- Do not overestimate the expected benefits versus the realities in order to [sell] the proposed change or initiative,
- Research best practice and measure its key elements against what is expected with the proposed change.
- Network with colleagues in and outside the organization
- Do literature search regarding best practices
- Use assessment tools such as; Pareto Principle, Fishbone diagram, Root cause analysis, etc.

❖ Build alliances that will be needed to support the proposed change
- Make sure leaders in other departments whose operations may be impacted by the proposed change are on board.
  - Be clear with the boss about the benefits and possible risks that may come with the proposed change.
  - Get assurance he/she will provide the resources that are needed.

❖ Recognize and account for the human element
- Communication, communication, communication
  - Multiple forms of communication may be appropriate.
    - o How will verbal and written notices and updates occur
- Be clear with employees about how the proposed change will impact them and account for reasonable losses they may perceive with the changes where possible

- Make provisions for maintaining two-way communication and identify who the project leaders will be.
- Establish reasonable time lines for accomplishing each milestone or way point during implementation
- Have clearly written procedures and operating instructions in place prior to implementation and ready for use.
- Be clear about additional or new employee competencies that will be required to perform tasks

❖ Project facilitators
- Select and empower facilitators who have both the people skills, personal drive, and competencies to provide on-site guidance during implementation.
- Be clear about the need for facilitators to understand and meet timeline objectives.
- Be clear about selection criteria for project leaders, managers, and facilitators

❖ Monitoring System
- Determine which monitoring tools are appropriate to measure progress at critical way points during planning and implementation.

❖ Build in opportunities to celebrate key accomplishments from planning through implementation. Celebrate a successful outcome with recognition to all and especially the key change agents.

❖ Conduct of project leaders
- Be clear, forthright, and accurate about information provided to employees
- Address or report rumors or discourse about the project directly, promptly, and appropriately
- Appropriately address issues of resistance or passive aggressive behavior by individuals or groups of employees.

Other Considerations

➤ Watch for Bumps and Cracks and Be Prepared to Take Corrective Action Early On
- Experiencing some "bumps" during implementation is a certainty no matter how perfect the plan may be. With proper planning these diversions are most likely to be minor. However, if serious unforeseen and validated obstacles develop, be willing to stop and quickly evaluate the situation rather than pressing on for the sake of time or discovery.

➤ Be Willing to Make Adjustments on the Fly
- Respond promptly when the monitoring tools indicate problems. Hoping problems will eventually resolve themselves will only lead to more complications and delays later. Project leaders and delegates who are overseeing the implementation phase of the initiative need to get together and find out what is happing, why, and take corrective action. In more extreme situations it may be necessary to halt or take necessary steps or delay various pieces of implementation until the situation can be worked out. Worse of all is ignoring the signs of trouble with the assumption things will work out.

➤ Establish and Exercise Alliances
- Good planning includes establishing key alliances throughout the organization with those who may be affected by a proposed change. Such alliances may be able to help reinforce the need for resources. Financial resources need to be defined and approved as early as possible while planning. Very often process changes in one department will impact or depend on operations in another. Establishing support from leaders in those departments is essential. Consider inviting people who represent those departments to participate in some way while planning. Here is where the lead change agent's reputation and management profile are especially important. If the project managers' profile is sufficiently high and trusted

by colleagues - problems that may arise can be more easily managed or avoided all-together.

➢ Establish simple Monitors that can Accurately Measure Progress in Real-time
- Easy to use and interpret monitoring systems are needed to track progress and untoward situations. They can be formal software applications or tools that were defined and developed by project leaders during planning. The essential point is planners need to identify key "way points" that signal real progress has been made.
- The number of these critical way points and how finely they are calibrated will vary depending on the size and complexity of the proposed change. Each way point needs to capture key events that are needed before managers can confidently claim "mission complete" for each stage of implementation.

➢ Find ways to Celebrate Milestones Reached Along the Way
- One of the fun things about initiating change comes with opportunities to celebrate successes such as meeting timelines. In addition to having well-deserved fun, these interim celebrations help to build pride among leaders and employees who are doing much of the hands-on work. Doing so helps to encourage everyone's best effort with the project.

➢ Maintain Strong Two-Way Communication Practices
- Good two-way communication signals to all involved that project leaders are not taking things for granted, which in turn, gives reason for all involved to feel a part of the project and encourages everyone to keep their eye on the ball. Efforts to maintain good two-way communication throughout planning and implementation.

A Final Thought

Several years ago, my boss offered a bit of advice and wisdom that proved to be useful over my years of management. He told me as I updated him with total confidence on a major department reorganization initiative, *the most dangerous time to ride a motorcycle is after you [think] you know how to ride it.* Implementing change in the workplace, no matter how clear the outcome may be envisioned, should be accompanied with an abundance of caution. The point is sometimes our enthusiasm encourages us to overlook signs that should be heated.

CHAPTER SUMMARY

➤ Make an accurate assessment of current operations
  o Complete a thorough fact-finding process
  o Validate assessments and double check assumptions
  o Define specific objectives the initiative is expected to achieve
  o Define a time line that is achievable for completing the needs assessment, planning, and implementation
  o Define the need for resources [money, people, equipment, supplies] and get assurances from senior management they will be available.
  o Be clear about how progress will be monitored from planning to implementation

➤ Create a draft of the proposed plan that addresses the key benefits and expectations of when implemented
  o Review the draft with managers and other key stakeholders
  o Make adjustments that are indicated
  o Develop alliances that may be needed

➤ Be clear about current competencies of employees and managers, and make provisions for training that may be indicated.
➤ Draft and re-draft the plan until all key elements are defined in sufficient detail
  o Work with line personnel who have hands on experience to be sure important details have been addressed

➤ Develop a process that will provide timely and ongoing communication among planners and those responsible for implementation.
➤ Make provisions to celebrate milestones that have been met
➤ Measure progress with easy to use tools that can provide timely and accurate tracking
➤ Measure outcome against criteria for success that has been defined in the plan

CHAPTER TEN

THE LION AND THE MOUSE

Once when a Lion was asleep a little Mouse began running up and down upon him; this soon wakened the Lion, who placed his huge paw upon him, and opened his big jaws to swallow him. "Pardon, O King," cried the little Mouse: "forgive me this time, I shall never forget it: who knows but what I may be able to do you a turn some of these days?" The Lion was so tickled at the idea of the Mouse being able to help him, that he lifted up his paw and let him go. Some

time after the Lion was caught in a trap, and the hunters who desired to carry him alive to the King, tied him to a tree while they went in search of a waggon to carry him on. Just then the little Mouse happened to pass by, and seeing the sad plight in which the Lion was, went up to him and soon gnawed away the ropes that bound the King of the Beasts. "Was I not right?"

said the little Mouse.

Little friends may prove great friends

CONCLUSION AND PRACTICAL APPLICATION

Knowing when to lead versus when to follow—*listening*—is a vital element for success.

CASE STUDY

Mary had been managing approximately two hundred employees for more than ten years in a division when Alison came on board as a senior manager to Mary's division. Mary's operation was relatively efficient, but employee turnover seemed high, and filling employee vacancies had been surprisingly difficult despite having a large pool of qualified talent in the surrounding communities. Employee complaints were low except for random issues that seemed to be resolved without difficulty. All the managers in Alison's management team worked well together, and in fact. Alison would occasional rely on Mary's long-term experience to get background information about operations in general and clues that could help address various issues.

One of Alison's practices had been to walk through her departments to say hello to staff and observe operations firsthand. These were casual visits, often not being more than five or ten minutes in each area. Conversations with employees and supervisors on these occasions ranged from, "How the day was going", to equipment issues, or perhaps hearing whose daughter just received a scholarship. However, after a number of these visits, Alison became increasingly aware of the type of responses to simple questions she was getting from Mary's employees. They were different from conversations with employees in her other departments. Here, employee responses seemed engaging but were truncated, and after a while, Alison began to sense something was missing in those brief responses. Alison also made a practice of sitting in at various department staff meetings and noticed attendance seemed much lighter at Mary's meetings. Also, there was less conversation and discussion. Conversation was mostly one-way. The meetings consisted mainly of Mary reporting on various matters with a short time given for open discussion, and not a lot of follow up items from previous meetings were covered.

After a few more months of these observations, Alison mentioned this to Mary, who became surprisingly defensive. With Alison's growing feeling that something more may be needed, she asked how Mary felt about scheduling an open discussion with her employees to talk about ideas or opportunities that could possibly improve operations or make their work easier to accomplish. The meeting was scheduled and had only moderate attendance. Some issues where discussed, but nothing appeared to be of major concern. Satisfied with the outcome, Mary felt better, but shortly after, an employee asked Alison's secretary for time to meet with Alison.

The employee was reluctant, but after getting an assurance of confidentiality, she explained her feelings to Alison about the work environment. She described Mary as a competent manager but one whose decisions were unpredictable and at times seemed to be very arbitrary. Further, she indicated it was not unusual for Mary to respond to an employee in a harsh manner that verged on being abusive. She said working in this environment made employees feel uneasy and sometimes feared for their jobs, especially if Mary felt challenged. The picture Alison had of operations started to focus a little more clearly, and Alison informed Mary of a meeting she wanted to schedule with the employees in her absence. At the meeting, a few employees who Alison recognized from her occasional walk-throughs as being reasonable and mature gave specific examples of their concerns. Alison came to the conclusion her feeling of uncertainty had grounding and were now supported by specific examples.

Alison talked with Mary about this afterward and asked Mary to re-evaluate her management style and consider her approach when handling various situations with employees, and asked for an informal improvement plan. A week later, Mary presented her plan to Alison, and while discussing the plan, two things became immediately evident to Alison. First, Mary had taken a decidedly defensive approach by minimizing her employee's feelings, and second it became clear that Mary was driven by a philosophy that showing flexibility and creating a measure of collegiality with her employees was a show of weakness. A weakness that she believed could be taken advantage of and lead to a loss of control. A short while after this meeting, a significant incident occurred with Mary and an employee in which Mary's handling could not be justified in any way. Other troublesome personnel management situations surfaced during the following few months. Alison considered Mary's long-term employment and continued to counselled Mary without seeing improvement. Eventually Alison asked for Mary's resignation. During the following weeks, Alison's actions appeared to be very much on track as anecdotes of how Mary exercised her authority and sometimes threatening demeaner surfaced.

DISCUSSION

In situations like these, it is critically important for the senior manger to maintain a balanced position when employees who report problems regarding their boss. On one hand as we saw with this case study, overlooking what may seem to be innocent or benign complaints from employees can support an unhealthy work environment. It seems employees always complain about their bosses, but sometimes these concerns are worth following up discretely. Exercising reasonable caution, commonsense, mixed with wisdom gained from past experience helps leaders assess these circumstances and balance what is only implied with the need to provide support to a manager.

To establish this balance senior managers need take the time needed to fact find and make a careful assessment. What surprised Alison initially was that Mary had held her position for many years without any apparent major difficulties. Yet, it became clear when suspicions were raised the work environment for her employees was not acceptable. Mary's employees liked their jobs and decided to work together under the circumstances to develop techniques and strategies they felt made the situation manageable.

Clearly, scheduling a meeting with employees without their supervisor or manager attending requires a great deal of caution. First, it must be discussed with the manager in advance and with very specific objectives for fact finding – not a process for encouraging accusations. If there are problems in the workplace, the manager or supervisor must be feeling associated stresses as well. The objective is to find ways to support Mary by discussing the issues and finding ways they can be resolved. Sometimes an outside facilitator can help with such a discussion, but in this case, Mary felt confident she could manage and maintain proper focus with the discussion. Once again, it's the issues that need to be discussed not individuals. If done properly these discussions can be viewed as help for the manager. In most situations the manager is not solely responsible all the problems. An open discussion conducted in as much as a [no fault] commentary as possible help define true cause and effect, and that is the first step to finding solutions.

CHAPTER SUMMARY

➤ Senior leaders should be open and willing to follow up concerns regarding managers who indicate underlying problems.
- o Be careful to not underestimate or overestimate a seemingly casual comment.
- o Ask questions discretely, secure other points of view regarding the concern.
- o If validated, proceed in a more direct manner for details.

➤ If process issues are sufficiently defined and validated, talk with the manager.
- o Get feedback and clarification from the manager
- o Consider extenuating circumstances that may be influencing the manager's conduct or approach.

➤ If concerns can be validated
- o Discuss ways improvements can be made
- o Define an action plan with timelines
- o Offer training opportunities to the manager

➤ Depending on the nature of the problem, consider getting assistance from HR counsellor and your boss.
➤ Track the individual's progress
- o Provide support with coaching and mentoring for management personnel.
- o This is a time for support and encouragement not accusations

➤ Move to counselling if sufficient progress is not made
- o Document progress with reasonable detail and in a timely manner.

➤ If the degree of progress is not acceptable continue with a higher level of disciplinary actions.

The discussions, suggestions, and strategies presented in this writing are not intended as panacea or "silver bullets" for finding solutions. They are intended to provide reliable and essential way points for exercising every day management responsibilities. The selected fables are intended to be a fun, useful, and easy tool that can help managers *remember* and use basic time-tested management principles - especially when confronted with difficult operations problems that have the potential to derail our thinking process.

The Oxen and the Lion

- Team Building: Effective operations are developed and sustained with strong leadership from a well-developed management team. The essential point for leaders is to provide clear standards of performance of individual managers, strong support and effective coaching and mentoring, and a clear vision of department operating standards.

The Mule and the Purchaser

- Management Competency and Hiring Criteria: A central and essential responsibility of leadership is to assess competencies of managers and provide opportunities to develop those skills and competencies. Operations become more efficient and employee morale can be strengthened when managers satisfy the two Dimensions of Management as defined in Chapter Two. The three key management traits [intellect, wisdom, and understanding] should be used to evaluate manager's potential to successful.

The Man, the Boy, and the Donkey

- Resolving Employee Conflicts: Effective and timely decisions can be made by defining clear boundaries for decision making and engaging employees in a process of exploring solutions.

The Eagle and the Arrow

- Verbal Communication: Practice preparing for formal and casual conversations with colleagues, employees, and upper management. Those speaking should satisfy their responsibility to present ideas clearly and in a manner that is best suited for the circumstances. The responsibility of those listening is to stay focused on the person speaking, what was actually said, and be willing to ask follow up questions to verify understanding.

The Boy and the Filberts

- Trying to Solve Too Many Problems: Attempting to solve multiple operations problems at the same time can be overwhelming. The initial step is to fact find each situation, decide which action plans can be packed together as one and which have to be implemented separately. Be careful about how the actions plans are sequenced.

The Mountains in Labour

- Finding Resolution to Long Standing Operations Problems: Having meeting about operations problems is not - taking action. Avoid meetings when valuable time is waisted with endless anecdotes that make the same point. Avoid discussions that are intended to divert making commitments that are needed to improve operations. Problems are almost never caused by a single element [person or situation] the objective is to get clarification on root cause and effect. Long term solutions come from action plans that are targeted to clearly defined performance standards and commitments from those in charge to meet those standards within reasonable timelines.

The Young Thief and His Mother

- Training to Meet Employee Performance Standards: Assessing employee competencies and providing ongoing training rather than employee counselling is often a more productive strategy for maintaining quality. There can be subtle slippage with employee skill level as new performance expectations evolve over time. Ongoing training encourages all employees to function at the level of their capability. Evaluate and update training programs and regimens as needed. Provide adequate training opportunities for employees.

Belling the Cat

- <u>Great Sounding Solutions are Often Not Doable:</u> Even the best sound solutions need to be thoroughly researched. The enthusiasm that often comes with moving ahead with a great idea can become very troublesome. Be aware of contingencies and assumptions the action plans are be based upon. If a proposed decision or action plan has more than two or more important contingencies, be cautious.

The Fox and the Goat

- <u>Look Carefully When Anticipating Operations Changes</u>: Making a careful and objective assessments of its value and feasibility will significantly improve success of outcome. Make sure stake holders and those who will be impacted by the change have appropriate opportunity to weigh in. Be wary of assumptions regarding the outcome that have not been carefully and thoroughly considered.

The Lion and the Mouse

- <u>Observe Subtleties</u>: Weight subtle comments about management personnel very carefully. A casual follow up assessment may provide validity. Take reasonable and appropriate steps to investigate while remembering an essential responsibility a leader has to his / her managers is provide support and guidance.